Phonics & Reading
Grades 2–3

Building Phonemic Awareness
And Early Reading Skills

By

Barbara Gruber, M.A. Ed.

Helene Chirinian, M.A. Ed.

Editors

Darcy Brown, Cynthia Holcomb

Copy Editors

Laurel Robinson

Debbie Shoffner

Gina Sutphin

Artist

Marilynn G. Barr

www.themailbox.com

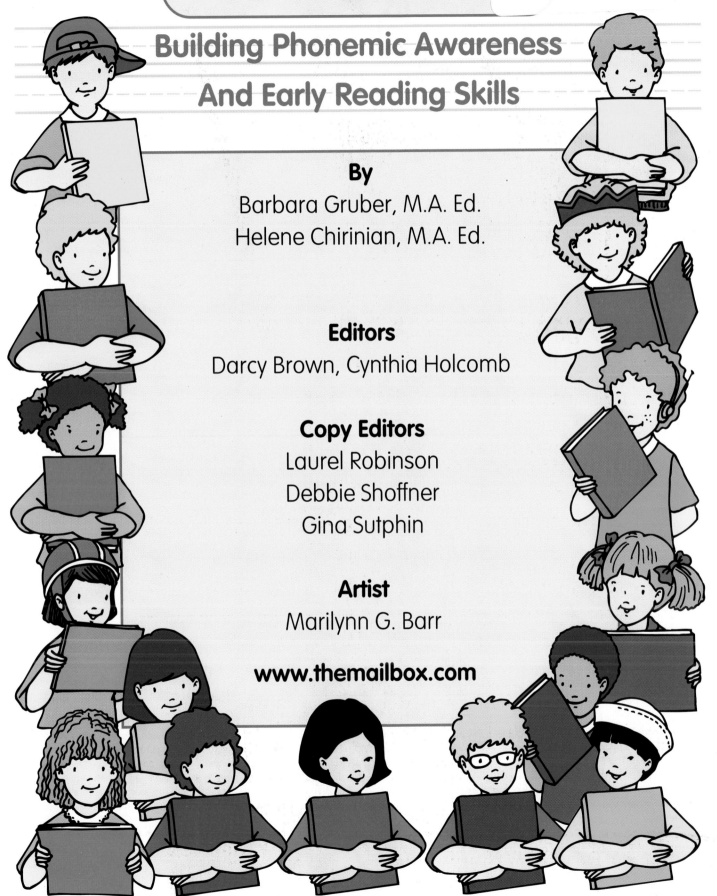

Manufactured in the United States

1 0 9 8 7 6 5 4 3 2

Table Of Contents

Why Should I Use This Book?

As teachers of second- and third-grade students, you are charged with the awesome responsibility of steering students' school careers in the right direction. Their days are packed with a variety of learning endeavors. But perhaps no aspect of teaching these young students is more rewarding than leading them on the adventure of lifelong reading.

This book is brimming with exciting teaching strategies and educational activities designed to strengthen your reading program and to enhance students' growth in phonics, phonemic skills, vocabulary development, and reading proficiency. These ready-to-use ideas are educationally sound and developmentally appropriate, and they require little preparation. They're just what a busy, dedicated teacher like yourself needs!

What makes this book different from other reading books?

This book is unique because it addresses both phonics and phonemic awareness. Phonemic awareness is the foundation upon which phonics skills are developed, and it is an essential component of successful reading programs.

Aren't phonemic awareness and phonics the same?

Phonemic awareness is the understanding that oral language is composed of a series of sounds. *Phonics*, on the other hand, is the relationship between oral and written language—translating sounds into print. Phonemic awareness is critical to the long-term effectiveness of phonics programs, specifically word recognition and spelling. Phonemic-awareness activities explore and manipulate sounds. These activities should be presented in a general progression, but the stages of phonemic awareness are not mutually exclusive. The phonemic-awareness skill areas (rhyming, alliteration, blending, segmenting, and manipulating sounds) complement each other and can be effectively woven together in lessons.

But what about my current program?

This book is designed to supplement, not replace, teachers' current phonics programs. It can easily be used in conjunction with any reading and/or phonics program. The pages are packed with practical, engaging activities that students will enjoy. The easy-to-use format will save teachers time by providing new and educationally sound activities. The book is conveniently divided into sections explaining how to establish a print-rich environment, involve parents, develop vocabulary, target high-frequency word skills, and keep students on the path to successful reading.

Where does literature fit into phonemic awareness and phonics?

Everywhere! Literature is an integral part of successful reading programs. Students need to be exposed to high-quality literature right from the start. Addressing phonics or phonemic-awareness skills in isolation is ineffective. Students need to learn that sounds are related to print and that print has meaning. This book recommends some wonderful literature to weave into the activities. With your modeling, students will also acquire knowledge of compound words, prefixes, suffixes, synonyms, antonyms, and other word skills. Even more importantly, they will be excited about reading!

What about writing?
When should I introduce it to my students?

Right away! Reading and writing are interrelated skills. Learning activities and suggestions for establishing a print-rich environment are provided throughout the book. With these tips and activities, you'll be well on the way to launching a successful reading program!

Setting The Stage

Plan for a successful reading program by transforming your classroom into a phonics-rich environment. The suggestions and reproducibles in this chapter will prove to be valuable building blocks for using the activities in this book.

Gathering Materials

Purchase inexpensive coloring books and calendars from discount stores, or ask parents to donate discarded calendars and picture books. These items provide a wealth of pictures for writing prompts. Sentence strips in a variety of colors are also useful for a number of phonics activities.

Place an assortment of pictures and sentence strips in a learning center. Encourage each student to write a descriptive sentence about the picture of his choice. For an added challenge, collect completed sentence strips and the corresponding pictures; then have your students match each sentence to the correct picture.

Integrating Phonics

Make phonics an integral part of your curriculum with the following suggestions:

- For a math-time merger, ask students to name the manipulatives they're working with. Create lists of vocabulary words with the named manipulatives and post them around the room.
- It's easy to integrate phonics into your social studies program. Themes—such as landforms, patriotic holidays, and community helpers—are loaded with vocabulary that can be learned using phonics. Make theme-related murals for your classroom walls by enlarging pictures with your opaque projector and tracing them on bulletin-board paper. Then have students name the objects in each picture as you record their responses on the papers. In the end, you'll have wonderful teaching tools for your social studies lessons, and your students will learn to identify the vocabulary words.
- Phonics activities can easily be incorporated into your science curriculum, too. As you introduce students to new animal, insect, plant, or other science-related vocabulary, have them identify prefixes, suffixes, number of syllables, and compound words. The number of opportunities you have to slip a phonics review into your teaching plans is limited only by your imagination.

Your Classroom Library

Setting up an effective and attractive classroom library is often the key to inspiring your students to read for pleasure. In addition to the books on your classroom bookshelves, add several new titles each week from the school or local library. Capitalize on your students' interests, holiday themes, and your current topics of study to help you in your selections. Then try some of these other hints for enticing students to use your classroom library.

- Provide fun and comfortable seating in your library corner. Place a beanbag chair, several large cushions, or carpet squares in your corner for students to use as they cozy up with books.
- Use baskets, plastic storage bins, or colorfully decorated boxes to store your books. Students will enjoy browsing through them to look for new books.
- Open a few books to interesting illustrations and put them on display. Clothespins can hold the books open. If desired, clip a caption or question to the open page to pique students' curiosity.
- Ask students to bring their favorite books from home to share with the class. Provide a special shelf for these books so your students will know these selections are featured on the recommended reading list!

Building Parent Partnerships

Involve parents in your phonics program. Once a month, or as often as desired, send parents a newsletter explaining their children's phonics progress, activities to use at home, and opportunities for parent participation. (If desired, use the newsletter reproducible on page 96.)

You can also invite parents to visit the classroom with a hobby, a collection, or a scrapbook to share with the class. Each parent has the potential to add to your students' vocabulary and background by sharing his interest with them.

Remind parents that literature is an important part of phonics development. Provide parents with lots of literature to use with their children—especially books that have alliteration, content vocabulary, chapters, or poetry. Place each book in a large resealable storage bag or in a bookbag with a note to parents. Send the bags home with students for weekend reading.

Goldilocks And The Three Bears

Princess And The Pea

Dear Parents

Build-A-Word Cards

These easy-to-make cards will become some of the most useful and most-used tools in your classroom. With a large set for you and smaller, individual sets for your students, you will be able to see immediately whether students understand the alphabet or phonics skills you're teaching. Each child manipulates his or her own set of cards and participates in the learning process. You may wish to laminate all the cards before cutting them out to ensure a longer life for them in students' hands.

If you prefer using pre-packaged cards, the following sets are available from The Education Center, Inc.:
- TEC816 Teacher Build-A-Word Cards
- TEC817 Student Build-A-Word Cards

Teacher Card Set

Duplicate tagboard copies of the blank "Teacher Build-A-Word Card Patterns" on page 17. Print each uppercase and lowercase letter of the alphabet onto separate cards using a thick black marker. If desired, use a different-color marker to write the lowercase letters to help children distinguish between the uppercase and lowercase cards more easily. Create extra cards for commonly used letters as needed. Laminate the cards for durability before cutting them apart. This set of cards will provide large, easily visible letters to use during whole-group instruction. They are also easy for students to hold and manipulate when participating in activities that require them to spell out words for whole-class lessons.

Storing Your Teacher Cards

Any number of methods can be used to store your cards. What you must anticipate is using them often, so you'll want to develop a system that makes it easy for you to use your cards in an instant. (You may want to put a rubberband around the uppercase and lowercase alphabets separately and keep them near your chalkboard.) If you've created several copies of each letter, you may want to store them in a shoebox or similar container that has file-folder dividers separating each letter set.

Using Your Teacher Cards

Because of the large size, your teacher Build-A-Word cards are easy to manipulate on the ledge of a chalkboard and can be easily seen by your students. When you're spelling only one word at a time, they will also work in a pocket chart if duplicated on tagboard. Individual students will also enjoy holding the cards for the rest of the class to view.

Build-A-Word
Cards

Student Card Sets

For each child in your class, make construction-paper copies of the "Student Build-A-Word Cards" on pages 12–16. If desired, use different-color paper for the lowercase and uppercase letters to help children distinguish the two letter types more easily. Create extra cards for commonly used letters as needed. If desired, laminate the cards for durability before having students cut them apart, or cut the sets on a paper cutter prior to giving the cards to students. This set of cards will provide easy-to-manipulate letters that children can use at their desks while you model words with your teacher card set.

Storing Student Cards

Any number of methods can be used to store student cards. You will need to decide which method works best for your classroom. You may choose to have each child keep a complete set of cards in an envelope in his desk. Or it may be more effective for you to store a class set of each individual letter in a resealable plastic bag. When you plan to work on a selected concept, you would give students only the letters they need to complete the lesson. Store the bags of letters in a shoebox or similar container.

Using Student Cards

The student Build-A-Word cards are a great way to provide students with a hands-on connection to phonics. Each time you model word examples with your teacher Build-A-Word cards, students can repeat the pattern on their desks using their personal card sets. For ease in handling, create card holders for your students from the description on page 10. Students can place their cards in the holders as they spell words; then they can raise the holders to show their work.

Card Holders For Student Build-A-Word Cards

Working with Build-A-Word cards on their desks, children learn to form new words. Here's a nifty card holder that will make it easy for students to keep their cards in order, manipulate them, and have them stay in place. It also makes it easy for you to see the results of each child's word-building efforts. The card holders are simple to make and easy to store in a box or file cabinet. Keep card holders at centers so children can build words during their free time or designated center times.

Creating A Card Holder

Use the following illustrations to create a card holder from a 9" x 12" sheet of tagboard or construction paper. Then repeat the steps to create a class supply. For durability, you may wish to laminate the paper before or after you've made the card holder. (If you laminate after it's created, you must reopen the pocket with a craft knife.)

Step 1:
Turn the paper horizontally and measure 2½ inches and 4 inches from the bottom on both sides. Make a mark at each measurement.

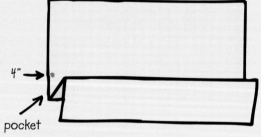

Step 2:
Make an accordion fold in the paper by creasing it at the 2½-inch marks and placing that folded edge at the 4-inch marks. You will form a pocket ³/₄-inch deep.

Step 3:
Staple on each side of the pocket to secure.

Pocket Charts

Pocket charts are perfect for many of the activities in this book—especially those involving the use of sentence strips. Store-bought charts are durable and look great, and if you have some, you can put them right to use. But if you want custom-made charts or if your school's budget is thin, you can easily make your own by following the steps below.

Pocket-Chart Construction

Determine the desired size of your chart by assessing your needs. Perhaps you need a small chart to use with individual word cards. Other times, a large chart may be useful for a short story written on sentence strips. Cut bulletin-board paper to the width needed, allowing extra length. If possible, laminate the paper before proceeding. Now make accordion folds in the paper to create the desired number of pockets. Fold the paper so that each pocket is about one inch deep. Allow space between the pockets to accommodate a sentence strip or other cards that you plan to use in the chart.

Essential Pocket-Chart Materials

To make the most of your pocket-chart instruction, it's helpful to keep some essential supplies on hand. Always keep a variety of sentence strips handy. Stock different colors and cut the strips to an assortment of lengths for different uses. A supply of index cards in different sizes can also be useful in your pocket charts. Also keep several markers nearby for quickly creating word cards and phrases.

Pocket-Chart Storage

Because of the variety of chart sizes, storing your charts can be a chore. Here's a handy way to store your charts and make them easily accessible. Punch two holes in the top of each chart and use metal rings to attach the chart to a clothes hanger. Hang the charts in your classroom closet. When you need a chart, it can easily be propped on an easel or chart stand, or you can use the hanger to hang it from a hook on your classroom wall.

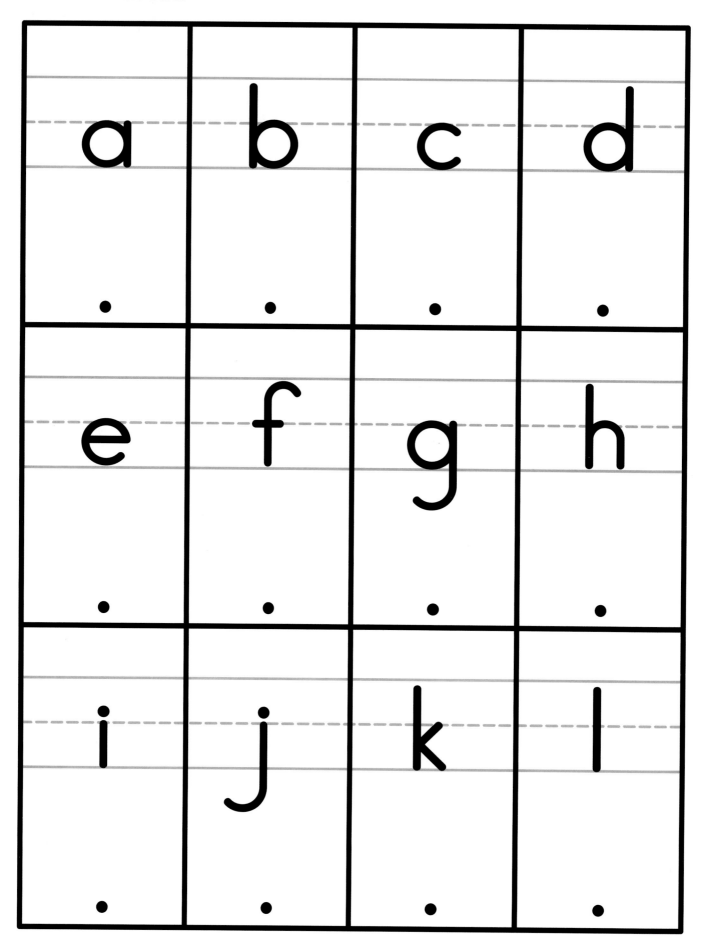

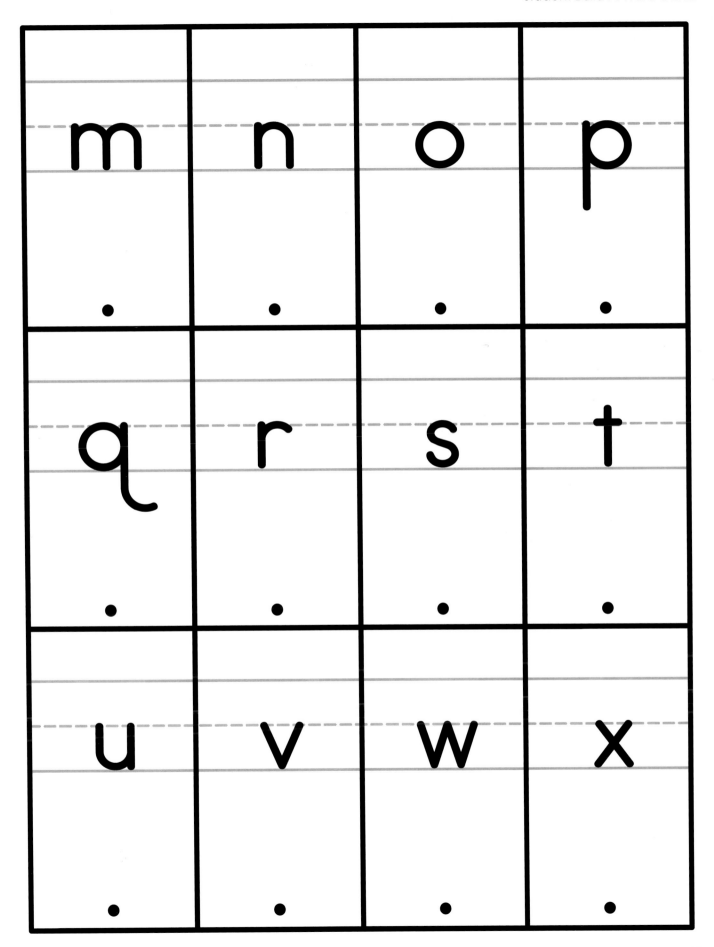

m	n	o	p
q	r	s	t
u	v	w	x

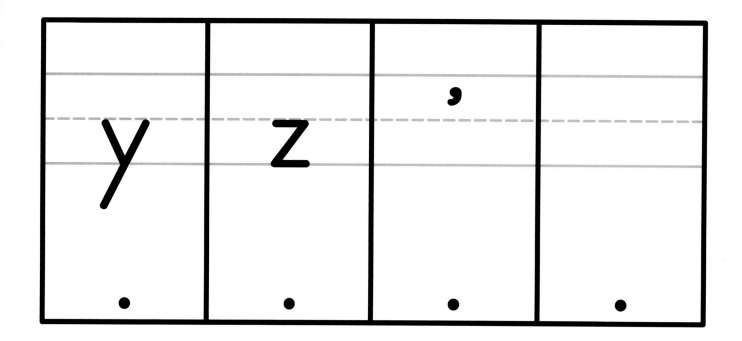

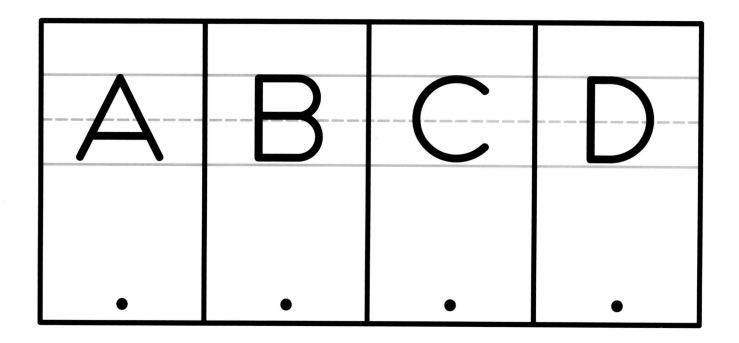

E	F	G	H
I	J	K	L
M	N	O	P

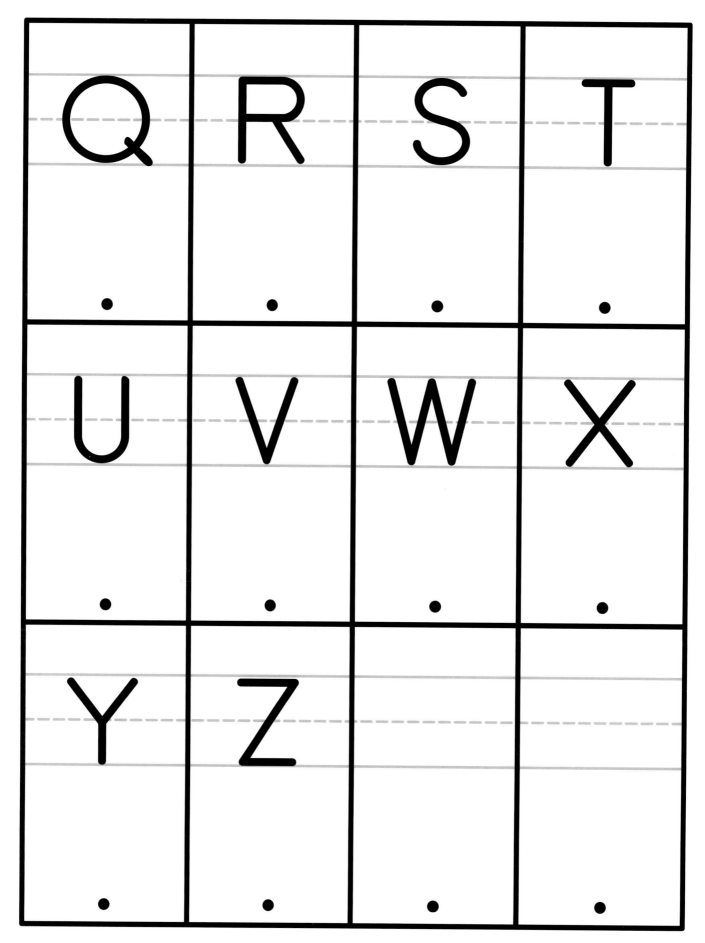

Using The Build-A-Word Cards

Word Chains

Use the Build-A-Word cards described on page 8 for this whole-group phonics activity. To begin, each student will need the following Build-A-Word cards:

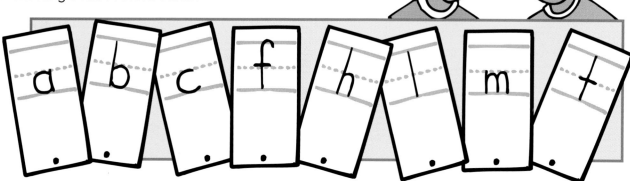

Ask students to separate their cards into vowels and consonants. Have student volunteers identify the group to which each letter belongs. Reinforce that the letters *b, c, f, h, l, m,* and *t* are consonants and that *a* is a vowel. Remind students that each word in the English language must contain at least one vowel sound; therefore, every word in the following activity will need to contain the letter *a.*

Tell your class that they are going to form words that contain the ending letters *at.* Have each student use her Build-A-Word cards to form the word *at* on her desktop. Explain that you are going to give clues about words that end with *at.* Students will use their Build-A-Word cards to form the word, say it aloud, and spell it aloud in unison.

Use the following examples to get you started:

Teacher: *Add a letter that will spell the name of an animal that meows. (Provide time for students to find the letter C and add it to the word.) What word did you make?*

Students: Cat; c, a, t.

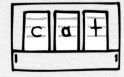

Teacher: *Remove the first letter. Now add a letter that spells something you can sit on. What word did you make?*

Students: Mat; m, a, t.

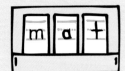

Teacher: *Remove the first letter and spell something you can wear. What word did you make?*

Students: Hat; h, a, t.

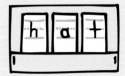

Continue the procedure as students spell other words in the family such as bat, fat, flat, and chat. Use the activity as desired to introduce other word families, practice spelling words, or reinforce phonics skills.

Using The Build-A-Word Cards

Word Whiz

This activity is a quick and easy one that can enhance a lesson or be used as a five-minute filler. Distribute a sheet of writing paper and a set of Build-A-Word cards to each student. Write a vocabulary word, a seasonal term, or the name of the month on the chalkboard. (A lengthy word will work best with this activity.) Have each student use his Build-A-Word cards to form the word on his desktop. Set a time limit and challenge the student to rearrange the letters to make as many different words as he can. Have the student list each word he makes. After the designated time period, have the students take turns sharing one word at a time from their lists. As a student shares a word, ask him to spell it aloud. Confirm the correct spelling; then ask all students who had the word on their lists to place a check mark by it. Continue having students share until all words have been checked.

What's The Word?

For a variation of the activity described at left, have students use their Build-A-Word cards to unscramble a mystery word. Secretly select a vocabulary word, a science term, or another pertinent word. Rearrange its letters as you write the word on the chalkboard. Instruct each student to use corresponding letters from his Build-A-Word cards to correctly spell the mystery word within a designated period of time. After that time, have a student volunteer identify and spell the word for the class. To extend the game, have that student select another word for the next round of play.

Using The Build-A-Word Cards

Spelling Squares

Challenge your students to look for spelling patterns with this small-group activity. To prepare, select nine letters from the Build-A-Word cards. Distribute a set of the letters to each group and a sheet of writing paper to each student. Instruct the students to arrange the Build-A-Word cards in a square as shown. The first player in each group must use two or more letters from the square to make a word. The other students check, and if the word is spelled correctly, the player writes the word on his list. He returns the cards to the square, and subsequent players take their turns. The player who has correctly spelled the most words after a predetermined amount of time is declared the winner for the round of play.

Scrambled Spelling

For a word review that will have your students on the move, play a few rounds of scrambled spelling! Write a list of spelling or vocabulary words on the board. Select the corresponding Build-A-Word letter cards needed to create the words. Mix the letters in a box and have each student draw one card. Instruct each student to work with other students to find the letters needed to spell one of the words on the board. When students complete a word, they should sit down in order so that their word is spelled correctly. After all students are sitting, call on each group to say and spell its word in unison for the class. Then have students return the cards to the box, where the letters can be scrambled for another round of play.

Using The Build-A-Word Cards

Say It Again!

Repetition can be the key to helping your children remember spelling patterns. This activity offers a creative way to practice vocabulary words, high-frequency words, or spelling words without written work. Use your class sets of the student Build-A-Word cards as described on page 8. Distribute a set to every student. Instruct each student to spell a specified word with his cards as you write it on the chalkboard. Then have the students look at their cards as they spell the word out loud in unison. Next, instruct each student to remove the first letter of the word and then spell the entire word in unison. Repeat the procedure, removing one more letter each time. Finally, after all the letter cards have been removed, have the class spell the word from memory. For a twist on the activity, place students with partners or in small groups to practice spelling a list of words.

Build It Back

Use a variation of the strategy described above to review for a spelling test or a vocabulary quiz, or as part of a daily drill. To prepare for the activity, gather your teacher set and the student sets of the Build-A-Word cards as described on page 8. Distribute a student set to each student and select the letters you'll need for the desired word from the teacher set. Display the word by placing the teacher cards on the chalkboard ledge, but omit a letter from the word. Instruct each student to spell the displayed word with the missing letter included. After students have had ample time to complete the task, place the missing letter card in its correct place so that students can check their work. Continue the procedure with other words from your list. For an added challenge, leave spaces for two missing letters, leave out all the vowels, or leave off the ending letter(s).

Can anyone identify the missing letter?

Building Words With Consonant

pl _uck

tr _uck

cl _ing

bl _ame

dr _ink

tr _ash

sh _ake

cr _ash

At this level, blends and digraphs are essential concepts that enable children to progress beyond "sounding out" single letters. By teaching children to recognize *blends* (consonant combinations in which you can hear each separate consonant) and *digraphs* (consonant combinations that form a new sound), you are helping them to become more fluent readers.

Hands-on word building helps students understand the way word parts work together. Your students can build words by combining blends and digraphs with rhyming phonograms (word families). Prepare for word-building activities by making sets of cards for the phonograms listed on page 23. Use a black marker to print each phonogram on a separate card. Then use a different color of marker to make sets of cards for the blends and digraphs listed on page 23. Be sure to use bold print and make the cards large enough so that they can be used with student groups. If desired, laminate the cards for durability so that students can also practice word building independently at their desks or in learning centers.

To engage the children in a word-building activity, distribute writing paper; pencils; and a set of phonogram, blend, and digraph cards to students placed in small groups. Instruct each group to place the phonogram cards in a pile and spread out the blend and digraph cards facedown. The first student removes the top phonogram card and selects one of the facedown cards. If the two cards make a word, each student in the group records the word on her individual sheet of paper. The blend or digraph card is then left faceup. Other students take turns selecting facedown cards to put with the phonogram, and if a word is created, it is recorded on their papers. After all blends and digraphs have been selected, they are returned to their facedown positions, and the next phonogram card is chosen for another round of play.

To extend this activity, give each student a supply of index cards. Instruct the student to write a different word from her blend and digraph list on each of her index cards. The resulting word cards can be used for alphabetizing practice, word recognition, identifying rhyming words, or classifying parts of speech.

sh _ame

pl _ate

sn _ake

bl _ack

gr _ate

cr _ack

tr _ack

Blends And Digraphs

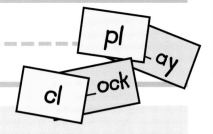

Super Sliders

Tachistoscopes, or word sliders, make enjoyable work out of word-list practice. Use the patterns on pages 24 and 25 to make construction-paper copies of seasonal or thematic shapes. Program each shape with a different phonogram. Partially fold the shape and make two horizontal slits in front of the phonogram as shown. Thread a paper strip programmed with blends and digraphs through the slits. Place the completed sliders in a learning center, or distribute them to individual students or student pairs for practice reading the resulting words. To extend the lesson, instruct each student to write sentences using the words on the sliders.

Phonograms				
ack	eat	ice	ock	uck
ail	ell	ick	oke	ug
ain	est	ide	op	ump
ake		ight	ore	unk
ale		ill	ot	
ame		in	own	
an		ine		
ank		ing		
ap		ink		
ark		ip		
ash		it		
at				
ate				
aw				
ay				

Beginning Consonant Blends

bl	cl	dr	fl	gl	pl	sc	tr
br	cr		fr	gr	pr	sk	tw
						sl	
						sm	
						sn	
						sp	
						st	

Digraphs

ch	sh	th	wh

Teacher Tip: When making the phonogram cards, write each phonogram close to the center of the card so that plurals and word endings also can be used.

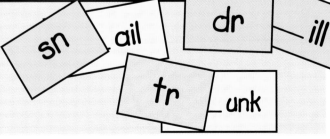

Patterns

Use with "Super Sliders" on page 23.

Go Fish—For Beginning Sounds!

Hook your students on blends and digraphs with this phonics version of the favorite card game Go Fish. To prepare for the game, select 13 blends and/or digraphs. Program decks of 52 colored index cards so that there are four cards of each blend and/or digraph in each deck. (Caution—make sure that the letters don't show through the backs of the cards!) To play the game, distribute a deck to a group of two to four students. The dealer distributes four cards to each player and places the remaining cards facedown in the center of the playing area. The first player asks another student for a letter combination to match one in his hand. If the student has the card, he surrenders it to the player, who then places the matching pair by his side. If the student does not have the requested card, he tells the player to "Go fish," meaning to take the top card from the pile in the middle. The game continues until all pairs have been matched. The player with the most matching pairs is the winner! For an added challenge, try some of the variations described below.

Do you have any "sh" digraphs?

• Have your students play Go Fish with one extra step: Before a player can lay a match down, he must say a word that begins with the blend or digraph on the pair of cards. The other players confirm the answer. If the word stated does not begin with the correct blend or digraph, the pair is placed at the bottom of the center pile of cards.

"sh" begins the word shark.

• Enlist your students in helping you prepare additional cards for the Go Fish deck. Assign a specific blend or digraph to each student. Distribute four index cards to each child. Instruct her to illustrate and label two pictures that begin with each of her assigned letters. Collect the cards and add them to your Go Fish decks, making sure that all the cards still have matched pairs. Have students play the game described above, giving each player the option of asking for a letter combination or a picture card during her turn.

"cl" can be found in clock, clown, clothes, and clam.

Blends And Digraphs

All-Star Folder Game

Provide a trail game for students to play to review beginning blends or diagraphs. Using a manila file folder and a marker, make a gameboard featuring five beginning digraphs or blends. (See the example shown.) Then make 20 picture cards—four different pictures for each blend or digraph. (A word list is featured on page 28.)

Explain the rules of the game as follows: Two players each select a penny to use as a game piece; one will be heads and the other will be tails. The first player draws a card and says the picture's name. He then moves his game piece, forward *or* backward, to the closest square in which the beginning letters appear. The game ends when all cards have been drawn. The player whose game piece is closest to the end is the winner.

Rhyming Review

Put a little rhyme into your beginning digraphs and blends review. To prepare, gather two colored markers, envelopes, and strips of tagboard (or index cards). Select five rhyming words that begin with different digraphs or blends. (See the examples below.) Make one card for each beginning digraph or blend; then, with a marker of a different color, make one card for the final letters common to all the words. Put each set of cards into an envelope, and place the envelopes, a supply of writing paper, tagboard strips, and a marker in a learning center. A student removes the cards from one envelope, spreads them out, and combines each beginning digraph or blend with the final-letter card. As the child makes each word, she prints it on a sheet of paper. Then, using her list of words, the student writes a rhyming couplet on a strip of tagboard. Post the couplets in a prominent classroom location for students to review.

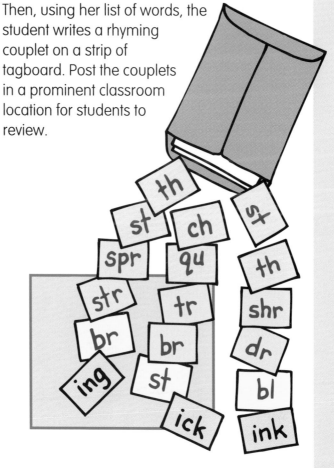

Activities For Using

Blend And Digraph Cards

Success is in the cards with a word deck that can be used in a variety of ways to reinforce blends and digraphs. To make a word deck, refer to the word lists below or create your own words that correlate to your current curriculum. (New words can be added to the deck throughout the year.) Use a marker to print each word on an index card; then, if desired, laminate the cards for durability. Use the completed word deck for the activities described on page 29.

Words With Blends

bl: black, blame, blanket, blink, block, blue

br: brain, brake, branch, brand, brick, bride, bridge, broom

cl: claim, clam, class, clean, clear, clip, clock, close, cloud

cr: crab, crack, cradle, crane, crayon, crib, crutch

dr: dragon, dream, drink, drip, drive, drool, dry

fl: flag, flame, flood, floor, flower, flute

fr: frame, free, freeze, fright, frog, fruit, fry

gl: glad, glass, gleam, glitter, glove, glue

gr: grain, grass, green, grill, grin

pl: plane, plant, plate, play, plow, plug, plus

pr: present, press, pretty, prince, princess, print, prize

sk: skate, skillet, skin, skirt, skull, skunk, sky

sl: slate, sled, sleep, sleet, slick, slide, slip, slope

sm: smack, small, smart, smile, smock, smoke

sn: snack, snail, snake, snap, sneak, sneeze, snip, snore, snow

sp: spare, speed, spider, spin, spirit, sponge, spool, spoon

spr: sprain, spray, spread, spring, sprinkle, sprout

st: stairs, star, start, stem, stick, stool, stop, store, stove

str: straw, stream, street, string, stripe, strong

sw: swallow, swan, swat, sweep, sweet, swim, swing

tr: track, trail, train, trap, tree, trick, trip, trunk

Words With Digraphs

ch: chase, cheat, cheese, cherry, chicken, child, chuckle

sh: shark, sharp, sheep, sheet, shell, shine, ship, shoe, shot, show

shr: shred, shrill, shrimp, shrink, shrub, shrug

th: thank, thimble, think, third, thirsty, thumb, thunder

thr: thread, three, thrifty, thrill, throat, throw

wh: whale, wheel, whine, whip, whisper, whistle

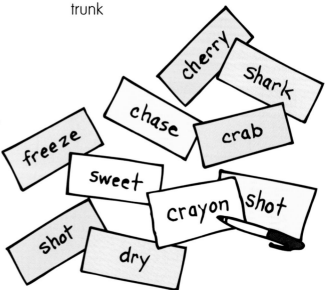

Blends And Digraphs

ABC Blends

Reinforce alphabetizing skills as your students review beginning blends and digraphs. Place students in small groups of three or four, and distribute an equal number of the word cards described on page 28 to each group. Instruct each group to work together to put the cards in alphabetical order. Check each group's efforts; then collect and redistribute the cards for additional practice.

brick

cherry

dry

freeze

plus

shot

thimble

wheel

Super Sentences

Incorporate sentence writing into this phonics practice. Distribute two word cards and a sheet of writing paper to each student. Instruct her to write a sentence that contains both words. Collect and redistribute the cards; then have students repeat the procedure. If time allows, ask each student to share her favorite sentence aloud with the class.

Team Spelling Bee

After students are familiar with the words in your word deck, use the cards for a spelling bee. Divide the class into two teams. Read the first word from the deck to the first player on Team One; then ask her to spell the word. If she is correct, her team is awarded a point. If she misspells the word, the first player in Team Two is given a chance to spell the word and earn the point. Continue the procedure, alternating teams, until each player has had a chance to spell a word. For a variation on the game, hold up a card for the player to read aloud. Points are awarded for each word that is read correctly.

Ending Blends And Digraphs

Repeat the activities using a word deck of ending blends and digraphs. Make a deck by using words from your vocabulary list, reading book, or spelling list. Have students look for words in newspapers or magazines, or lead a student brainstorming session for words to include in the deck.

Phonics Games

Your students will be eager for phonics reinforcement when it's presented in a fun-to-play format. Refer to the following ideas for games that will help review important phonics skills as well as provide activities for five-minute fillers or indoor fun for inclement-weather days.

Crossword Puzzlers

Weekly spelling words won't seem puzzling after this practice activity. In advance, make an overhead transparency of a sheet of centimeter graph paper. For each spelling word, arrange empty boxes in a crossword-puzzle fashion on the transparency. Number the boxes on the transparency to show how the words will fit together. Project the image onto a dry-erase board or sheet of bulletin-board paper. Provide a context clue about each word for your class. Have student volunteers use a marker to write the correct letter in each box. For added enrichment, have the students write the context clues for you to read aloud.

Phonics Bingo

This practice for letter/sound association can be used with beginning sounds, ending sounds, digraphs, blends, rhyming words, or vowel sounds. To prepare, visually divide a class set of 6" tagboard squares into nine boxes—three rows across and three rows down. Program each box with a letter, letter combination, or word correlating to the desired phonics skill. (Note that each card in the set should have the same letters, but they should be placed in different boxes on the cards.) Next prepare one set of large picture or word cards that correspond to the letters in the programmed boxes.

To play the game, distribute a supply of game markers—such as beans, pennies, or construction-paper squares—and a gameboard to each child. Place the picture (or word) cards in a pile. Turn over the top card and show it to the students. Have the children find the letter on their gameboard that matches the picture or word card displayed. Children may place only one marker on their bingo card for each picture or word shown. The first player to place three markers in a row—horizontally, vertically, or diagonally—is the winner.

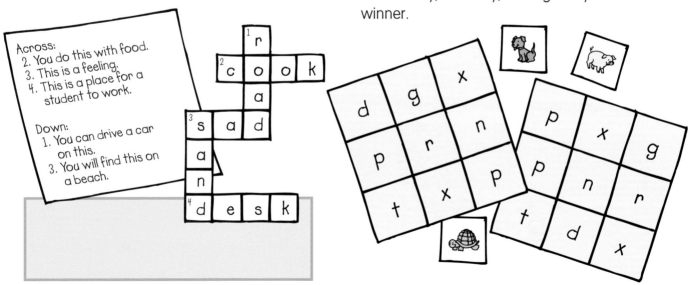

Across:
2. You do this with food.
3. This is a feeling.
4. This is a place for a student to work.

Down:
1. You can drive a car on this.
3. You will find this on a beach.

Rhyme Toss

Your students will love this fast-paced game that reinforces rhyming words. Gather your students in a circle and toss a small foam ball to a child. As you toss the ball, say a word that the student will have to rhyme. If he correctly names a rhyming word, he then says a different word, and tosses the ball to another student. This student then repeats the procedure. If he makes an incorrect response, he tosses the ball back to you, and another student has a chance to catch it and name a rhyming word. Continue until all students have participated, or as time allows.

You can adapt the tossing game to reinforce vowel sounds, blends, or digraphs. Simply state a desired skill aloud. Give students an example of the skill. Then toss the ball to a student. The youngster who catches it must respond with a word containing the specified letter or letter combination. To reinforce antonyms or synonyms, say a word as you toss the ball. The student who catches it must name a word with the same or opposite meaning.

Twenty Questions

Turn an all-time-favorite game into an entertaining way to reinforce phonics. Announce a vowel sound, letter blend, or digraph as the topic of the game. Explain to the children that the word you are thinking of contains a certain letter(s). To help identify the word, the students may ask you questions that can be answered only by yes or no. They may ask a total of 20 questions, with the object being to guess the word in 20 questions or less. When a student correctly identifies the word, he may come to the front of the room and secretly select a new word for another round of play.

31

Rhyme Time

This word game is perfect for reinforcing spelling words or practicing phonetic skills. Post your weekly spelling words (or words to be reviewed) for students to refer to. Invite your students to sit in a circle. Secretly select one of the words on the list and give a clue such as, "It rhymes with 'car' but begins with the *st* blend." The student to your left guesses the word. If he is correct, he gives a clue for another word on the list. If he is incorrect, the child to his left guesses the word. Play continues around the circle until all words on the list have been used, or all students have had a chance to participate.

It rhymes with 'car' but begins with the *st* blend.

Weekly Spelling Words

stop	who
star	he
come	she
run	from
went	stay

Alphabetical Relay

Students will be on the move with this action-packed game! Program a class set of index cards with vocabulary words, spelling words, or individual letters. Divide your class into four teams and distribute a card facedown to each student. At your signal, each student looks at her card and arranges herself in alphabetical order with her teammates. After a desired amount of time, call for students to "freeze" in place. Check the order of the cards, and if students are arranged alphabetically, their team earns one point. Collect the cards and redistribute them for another round of play. Continue the game until a team has earned ten points and is declared the winner.

face   made   save   tame

For added enrichment, have the entire class line up alphabetically before you collect the cards after the final round of play. Or, if desired, ask each student to use her word in a sentence or to name a word beginning with the initial letter on her card.

Spell-Tac-Toe

This spelling game will add flair to traditional spelling practice. To play the game, draw a tic-tac-toe grid on the chalkboard. Divide the class into two teams and assign one team X and the other O. Explain to students that their team earns the chance to spell a word by first identifying the number of letters (or syllables) it has. Call out a word to the class. The student who is first to raise her hand and correctly announce the number of letters (or syllables) in the word may spell the word for her team. If she spells the word correctly, she marks her team's symbol on the tic-tac-toe grid. If she misspells the word, the other team has the opportunity to spell the word. After a player has had a turn, she must wait until all team members have participated before she volunteers another answer. Continue the game by alternating between each team, using words from the list. Several tic-tac-toe games can be played so that all the weekly spelling words are reviewed.

"Birthday" has two syllables.

Vocabulary Bingo

A round of bingo provides an enjoyable way for students to review their vocabulary list. Each time a new vocabulary list is introduced, have students prepare a bingo card to correspond with the list. To make a bingo card, distribute a sheet of white paper to each student. Have students fold their papers four times to create 16 squares. Have them unfold the papers and trace over each crease with a pencil or black crayon. Instruct each student to write his name in one square (to be used as a free space), and a vocabulary word in each of the remaining squares. (If the vocabulary list contains more than 15 words, allow each student to select which words he will leave out. If the list has fewer than 15 words, add enough review words to the list to fill the squares.)

When the game cards are complete, distribute dried beans, paper scraps, or chips to use as markers. Call out the definition of one of the vocabulary words. If the student has the matching term on his card, he covers it with a game marker. Continue to call out words until a student has bingo, or four covered spaces in a row. The student must then use each of his covered words in a sentence. If he uses them correctly, ask him to be the caller for the next round of play.

Teacher Tip: You may want to keep the previously used bingo cards on file for an instant review of past vocabulary words.

Wonderful Word Walls

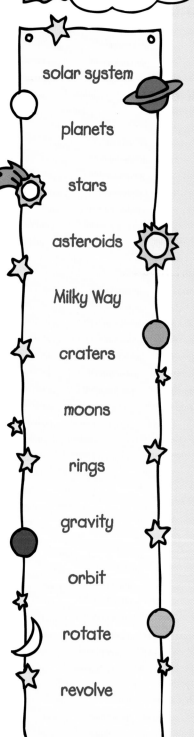

solar system

planets

stars

asteroids

Milky Way

craters

moons

rings

gravity

orbit

rotate

revolve

comet

Look out—word walls are popping up in classrooms everywhere! A word wall is a fun and functional way to help your youngsters read, spell, write, and practice phonemic awareness. There are so many wonderful ways to create and use word walls that you may want to have several on display in your classroom. Read the suggestions below for creating and using word walls with your students; then enjoy the many activities that can be incorporated with this unique learning tool!

How Do You Make A Word Wall?

As simple as the name sounds, there's more to creating word walls than just taping word cards to the wall! To create a word wall in your classroom, you first must determine the needs and ability levels of your students. For beginning readers, your word wall display could include illustrated word cards or picture cues grouped according to beginning sounds. High-frequency words are also a good choice for this type of display. For more fluent readers, try creating word walls for phonograms (word families), frequently misspelled words, new vocabulary, and science or social studies terms. Let the needs of your youngsters and the subject of your studies direct the selection of words for each classroom display.

Where Do You Place A Word Wall?

Word walls should be placed in the highly visible areas of your classroom. Students should easily be able to see each display so that they can refer to it throughout the day. When you select a spot for a word wall, give it a "test drive" by sitting in different areas of your room to ensure that it will be accessible to each student. Bulletin boards are excellent places to create word walls, but paper banners attached to the walls, doors, and cabinets in your classroom can work just as well. Seasonal cutouts can be programmed with words to make a decorative yet functional display. And if you have a section of your chalkboard to spare, put it to good use by writing a list of words for students to observe. Where should you place a word wall? Wherever you find need for one!

Wonderful Word Walls

When Do You Add Words To Your Wall?

Put words on your wall displays in the context of language activities. Post one or a few words at a time. Discuss with your students why the word is being placed on the wall: it may belong to a word family, appear in a new story, or have a content-related meaning. If the word is being added to an existing word wall, ask students to surmise why the new word belongs to a specific display. If the word is the beginning of a new word wall, have students predict other words that might eventually be added to the group. Adding a word to a wall display should include plenty of student interaction—the more involved the students are with the words, the more meaning they will gain from the word wall experience.

Why Are Word Walls Valuable?

Word walls are a great starting point for many phonemics-rich activities. They serve as a reference for students who need additional exposure to reading vocabulary and spelling words. They also provide a continual review of words studied throughout the year. And when it comes to student writing, these word walls provide a wonderful vocabulary resource for children to use in their work. The ideas on the following pages describe other specific uses for these word-rich displays. After using them in your classroom, you'll find that word walls are an invaluable teaching tool!

Who Adds Words To The Word Walls?

Of course your curriculum will determine many of the words that belong on the classroom word walls. But why not set up a word wall for students to build as they find words from independent reading, current events, and special-interest vocabulary? Set aside a special time each week for students to discuss interesting words they have come across and would like to share with the class. Then write the word for each student volunteer and invite him to place the word card on this special display.

Wonderful Word Walls

Hands-On Word Walls

For an interactive word wall, a simple step can change a stationary display into a hands-on learning center. This activity works best with a word wall that is mounted on a sheet of poster board or is attached to a bulletin board covered with heavy background paper. Use an X-acto® knife to cut small slits in the background paper or poster board and insert a paper clip through each slit. Word cards can be slipped under the paper clips, making them easy to remove for activities such as alphabetizing, classifying nouns and verbs, and arranging by number of syllables. You can also program a definition on the back of each card and have students participate in a self-checking of their understanding of each word.

Another type of interactive word wall can be made by attaching a strip of magnetic tape to each word card. The cards can be manipulated on a magnetic chalkboard, filing cabinet, or other magnetic surface. When word walls double as learning centers, your students will get twice as much use from them!

Teacher Tip: Extend the concept of interactive word walls with Word-Wall-In-A-Box! As you add a new word to your wall, make a duplicate card to place in a file box. This box of duplicate word-wall cards comes in handy for alphabetizing practice, word games, and individual student practice. The extra cards take only seconds to make and allow the words to be manipulated if it is not convenient for them to be removed from the wall.

Wonderful Word Walls

Spelling Words On The Wall

A word wall can be a big boost for studying the weekly spelling words. Designate a special word wall specifically for spelling words studied throughout the year. As new words are introduced, write each word on a card for students to observe. Ask your students to determine how many syllables each word has, if it contains any prefixes or suffixes, or what its definition is. Then have students guide you as you attach the word cards to the wall in alphabetical order. Leave the new words on display all week; then cover or remove them during the spelling test. After the test is over, put the words on permanent display along with words from previous spelling tests.

Teacher Tip: Write each week's spelling words with a different-colored marker or on a certain color of index cards. Use the color code for review purposes. You can instruct students to study all the words written in a certain color and then have an oral spelling quiz on those words.

Word-Families Word Wall

Your students will be amazed at all the words that can be made with just a few phonograms. Refer to the list of phonograms on page 23. Each week select several phonograms to feature on a word wall. Working with one phonogram at a time, ask your students to brainstorm a list of words that can be made with the ending letters. Make a word card for each correct response. If desired, have the students work together to arrange the words in alphabetical order. Then attach the cards under the corresponding phonogram as shown.

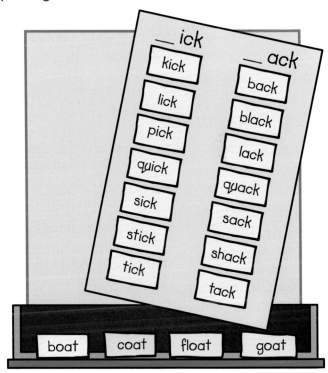

Teacher Tip: The chalk ledge is a great spot for alphabetizing. Spread out the word cards and have students guide you in arranging the words in the correct sequence.

Wonderful Word Walls

More Word Wall Activities

Get more mileage from your word walls as you incorporate these student-pleasing activities. By having your students move, chant, and interact with the words, you'll provide a vital kinesthetic link for young learners.

Point And Spell

Use a pointer to reinforce spelling with a rhythmic touch. Say a word from your word wall; then point to each letter with your pointer as you spell the word aloud. If possible, chant the letters to make the spelling have a rhythmic pattern. Then have your students join you in repeating the word and its spelling. To add student interest, have different student volunteers point to the letters as the class spells each word from the wall aloud.

Step And Jump

Get your students on the move with this spelling activity. Point to a word on a word wall and say it aloud. Have students jump in place as they repeat the word. Next have them march in place, taking one step each time they say a letter in the word. Then have them jump as they say the word again. Vary the activity by having students snap instead of jump, clap instead of march, or whisper the words.

Write It In The Air

What's the good news about writing words in the air? The pencils never break or need sharpening, you never run out of paper, and the children love it! Point to a word on a word wall and have the students say the word aloud. Next instruct the students to "write" the letters of the word in the air as they spell the word in unison. Then, just for fun, have each student "erase" the letters before you point to the next word.

Wonderful Word Walls

Mystery Words

Your students will love this guessing-game approach to spelling words from the word wall. Ask your students to close their eyes while you turn ten of the words into mystery words by using self-stick notes to cover several letters in each word. Have your students open their eyes; then call on volunteers to identify the covered letters in each word. After the letters in a word are correctly identified, remove the self-stick notes and have the class spell the word in unison.

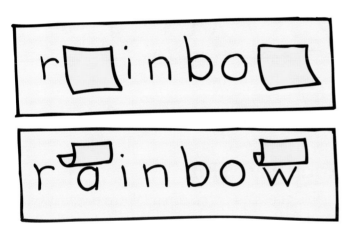

Colorful Word Shapes

Have students practice writing words in color from the word wall. Instruct each student to copy designated wall words on paper. After he copies a word, the student draws around the word's shape in crayon as shown. For added reinforcement, instruct him to select two more crayons to use as he outlines the word twice more. If desired, ask students to compare words that have similar shapes.

Write And Trace

Try this variation of the pencil-and-paper routine. Point to a word on the word wall and have students write it on a sheet of paper as you spell it aloud. Next have each student use a crayon to trace over each letter in the word as she repeats the spelling. Finally have the student underline the entire word as she says it aloud.

39

Wonderful Word Walls

Sort It Out!

This sorting activity reinforces classification skills while promoting word recognition. Remove a desired number of words from a word wall. Then ask your students to sort the words by one of these attributes:

- the number of letters in each word
- the number of syllables in each word
- the parts of speech
- the beginning/ending letters
- vowel sounds
- beginning/ending blends
- singular/plural
- vowel combinations

After sorting, have all students say the word on each card as you replace it on the wall.

Sort these words by the number of letters in each word.

at

fun

little

can

should

is

Something In Common

Prepare for this critical-thinking game by removing words with a common attribute from a word wall. (For attribute ideas, see the list above.) Display the words on the chalk ledge or another place for easy viewing. Ask your students to determine what words in that group have in common. When a student correctly identifies the attribute, have her secretly share with you an attribute for the next round of play.

The words are adverbs!

sadly quietly slowly quickly

Read My Mind

This guessing game can reinforce a variety of word skills. Tell your students that you are thinking of a word from the word wall. Supply them with its definition and ask the students to "read your mind" by identifying the word. The students may scan the wall for a word that matches that definition. Once the correct word is identified, point to the word and have students say it in unison. You can also ask students to read your mind for words that are synonyms, antonyms, or rhyming words.

I am thinking of a word from the word wall ...

Wonderful Word Walls

Word Wall Assessments

For a quick quiz, a mastery check, or a weekly assessment, you'll find that your word wall comes in quite handy. You can assess students individually or as a group by having them read aloud new vocabulary words, identify rhyming words, or name ten words containing a specific vowel sound. For quick written assessments, instruct your students to number their papers and refer to the wall to find the matching answers as you call out definitions, synonyms, or antonyms. You can also have students write sentences with designated words from the wall to evaluate their understanding of using the words in context. Or, if desired, write sentences on the board, leaving blanks where vocabulary words should be. Have students search the wall for words that make sense in the blanks.

You'll find that word walls are also very helpful to students who need tutoring or additional reinforcement in language arts. The format for using the word walls will be familiar to the students, and you won't need to spend time preparing additional materials for these learning sessions. In addition, the words you review will be on display the entire day for students to refer to.

The possibilities are many, and your wall will save you time in preparing both assessment and tutoring materials. Best of all, the word wall will be ready whenever you are!

Teacher Tip: Use a different color of marker or index cards for each new set of word cards. When it comes to assessment time, you can simply ask students to refer to words of a certain color.

Good Morning.

Please find ten 2-syllable words and write them on your paper.

1. happy
2. tiny
3. open
4. quiet
5. pretty
6. lion
7. tiger
8. over
9. under
10. into

The boy jumped very high.

The little tiger went for a walk.

little

jump

could

did

big

went

over

Working With Word Skills

In addition to learning the basics of phonics, students need plenty of exposure to word concepts such as root words, prefixes, suffixes, compound words, and contractions. The following activities will make practicing these concepts enjoyable for your students as you reinforce the word skills that are essential for fluent readers.

Prefixes And Suffixes

Prefixes and suffixes are additions to root words that change the meanings of the words. *Prefixes* are added to the beginning of words, and include *de-*, *dis-*, *pre-*, and *mis-*. *Suffixes* are added to the end of words and include *-ing*, *-ment*, and *-ly*. Students in the primary grades can easily learn prefixes and suffixes by adding them to words they already know. Refer to the lists on page 49 for commonly used prefixes, and suffixes and their meanings.

Using Prefixes And Suffixes On Your Word Wall

Prefixes and suffixes can easily be added to the words on your word wall. Make word cards featuring the desired prefixes or suffixes. (These cards should be a different shape or color than the root words to help students distinguish them.) Invite your students to place the prefix cards in front of the words already featured on the wall. If the prefix and root word form a new word, attach the prefix card in front of the root word. Discuss the meaning of each newly formed word before testing other words.

Repeat the procedure for suffixes by having students add suffix cards to the end of words displayed on the wall. Reinforce the meanings of the newly formed words by having each student use one of the new words in a sentence.

Prefix Line-Up

Give each student a 5" x 7" card programmed with a prefix, a suffix, or a root word. Have all the students with a root word stand in a line. Instruct the students with prefixes and suffixes to stand by a root word. When all students are correctly paired, ask each student in the pair to devise a sentence using the new word.

Let's review our spelling words.

The story was mostly nonsense.

Working With Word Skills

Mix 'n' Match

This enjoyable way to teach prefixes and suffixes has success in the cards! Write several prefixes or suffixes on separate index cards or tagboard squares. Next program cards with root words that fit the prefixes or suffixes. Spread the cards on a table and have student pairs take turns matching the word parts to the root words. When a correct match is made, have the students create a sentence with the word, then write it on a sheet of paper. Post the completed sentences for other classmates to observe.

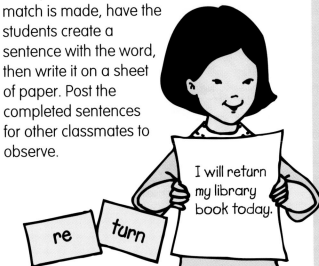

Prefix Patrol

Provide practice with dictionary skills as you send your students on a search for prefixed words. Assign a prefix to each pair of students and provide them with a dictionary and three notecards. Have partners work together to find three words with their designated prefix. Instruct the pair to write each word on a separate notecard. When the class is ready, call on the pairs to share their findings. After the partners share their words and their meanings, the pair calls on classmate volunteers to use each word in a sentence. After all words have been shared, add the word cards to an existing word, wall or create a new display for the prefixed words.

Suffix Flip Booklets

Students will flip over these word-building booklets! To make a booklet, each student will need one 2" x 5" strip of tagboard and several 2" x 2" squares of tagboard. Instruct the student to write a specified word on the left half of the longer strip. Have the student brainstorm for possible suffixes to add to her word. Verify the spelling and correctness of the results before having her write one suffix on each of the shorter cards. After the student writes each suffix, assist her in stacking and stapling the squares to the end of the longer strip as shown. (Make sure to leave a blank square on top of the stack.) Provide time for students to share their completed booklets in a small-group setting; then store the booklets in a learning center for students to review during independent learning time.

Working With Word Skills

Clever Contraction Cut-Ups

Engage your youngsters in making learning materials for the classroom as you reinforce contraction word skills. To participate in the project, each student will need a 5" x 7" piece of construction paper. Instruct each student to fold her paper in half lengthwise and cut a slit through one half as shown. Post a list of contractions (a reference list is provided on page 50). Direct each student to select a word from the list and write it on the uncut portion of her paper. Next have her fold down the cut sections and write the two words that form the contraction (see example). Place students in small groups to share their handiwork with their classmates. Then store the finished projects in a learning center for additional practice with identifying contractions.

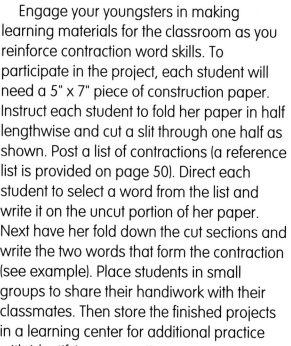

Contraction Quest

Reinforce contractions by sending your students searching for words. Gather a supply of magazines and newspapers, and tear out individual pages or articles. Distribute a page to each student and challenge him to find and circle as many contractions as possible. Next have each child write the two words that make up each of his circled contractions on a sheet of paper. For an added incentive, place additional pages in a learning center, and keep a record of who has identified the most contractions.

The Contraction Corner

Keep your students on the lookout for contractions with this simple activity. Each morning, announce a contraction of the day. Have your students look for the specified contraction in their reading books, science texts, library books, or other sources they encounter throughout the day. When a student finds a contraction, invite him to write it on the chalkboard in a designated area called "Contraction Corner." Review the list at the end of each day.

Tactile Contractions

For a tactile approach to contraction practice, supply each student with a plastic bag filled with alphabet-shaped cereal or pasta and small-sized elbow macaroni. Instruct each student to use her letters to spell contractions, using the elbow macaroni for apostrophes. If desired, have the students glue their words to index cards. Pair students to check the word cards for correct spelling, or place the cards in a learning center for independent review.

Working With Word Skills

Seasonal Compound Word Puzzles

Provide a vocabulary-building review of compound words with a learning center that changes with the seasons. To prepare for the activity, have students brainstorm a list of compound words relevant to the current season. Place the list, a supply of seasonal cutouts, scissors, and colored pencils in a learning center. Invite each student to visit the center and write a word from the list on a seasonal cutout. Next have the student illustrate the word on the back of the cutout; then have him cut apart the word in puzzle-piece fashion, separating the individual words of the compound. (Remind each student to place a check mark on the list next to the word he selected so that there are no duplications.) Store the completed puzzle pieces in a decorated envelope for students to assemble as they visit the center to review the seasonal compound words.

Compound Word Posters

Initiate a student-driven review of compound words by having your class create word posters. Place students in small groups and supply them with large pieces of construction paper and markers. Assign each group a word, such as *fish, sun, snow,* or *bird.* Challenge each group to think of as many compounds as possible using its words. Provide time for each group to share its word list with the class before you display the completed posters in your classroom.

starfish
catfish
goldfish
sunfish
fishbowl
fishnet

Picture Puzzle Compounds

Add an artistic touch to your study of compound words. Divide the class into groups, each of which is to create picture cards for compound words. Instruct each group member to list compounds whose two words can be shown by pictures. (A reference list is provided on page 51.) Provide each group with tagboard cards and markers. Have each student make a card by illustrating two pictures that represent one of the compound words from her group's list. Next have her code the back of the card with the corresponding compound word. Then have the groups exchange cards and solve the picture puzzles.

Working With Word Skills

Understanding Plurals

Invite your students to become word detectives as they deduce how to make words *plural*, or show that there is more than one. Introduce four categories for plural words as follows:

• words that add -s to the end: *tree, hat, dog, plant*
• words that add -es to the end (mostly words ending in *ch, sh, ss, x*. When -es is added, a new syllable is usually created): *dish, fox, lunch, glass*
• words that add -ies to the end (words that end in y; the y is changed to an *i*): *candy, puppy, party, pony*
• irregular plurals: *foot, goose, tooth, man*

Post a list of words, such as *girl, cup, dress, bench, baby, penny, mouse,* and *child*. Ask your students to determine the spelling of the plural form of each word and state the reason for the spelling.

Plurals In A Row

Reinforce plurals with a fun game of tic-tac-toe. Prepare a gameboard by writing the singular form of nouns on a grid (see example). Pair students, then provide each pair with a copy of the gameboard. Have one student choose a word from the grid and write its correct plural form on a separate sheet of paper. Have him mark an X (or an O) over the word for a correct answer. Then it is his partner's turn. The first player to mark three nouns in a row is the winner. Encourage the winner to help his partner complete another row of plural nouns correctly.

Plural Riddles

Provide additional practice with each type of plural with a riddle-writing activity. Give each child a plural noun with the desired spelling rule to reinforce. Have her write a riddle for which her word is the answer, such as "You use one kind of us to paint and another kind to clean your teeth. What are we?" *(brushes)* If time allows, have the students share their riddles with their classmates. Ask student volunteers to spell the answers as they try to solve each other's riddles.

We are round and brown. A pair of us is worth two cents. What are we?

pennies

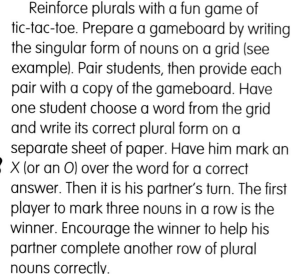

cat	glass	dish
fox	mouse	clock
book	bench	foot

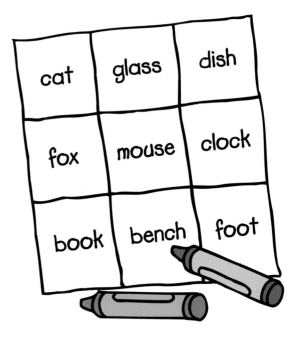

Working With Word Skills

Homophone Happenings

Reinforce homophones with a student-generated reference box for these sound-alike word pairs. List several homophone pairs such as *dear/deer*, *our/hour*, and *eight/ate*. (Refer to the list on page 52 for additional homophones.) Point out to your students that the words sound the same but have different spellings and meanings. Ask your students to use these words in context as you record each sentence pair on a sentence strip. Display the sentences on the chalk ledge or in a prominent location for several days; then store the strips in a box labeled "Homophone Happenings." Encourage student pairs to read the sentences in the box during free time or for reading reinforcement.

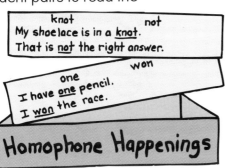

Tracking Down Homophones

Use student-created stories to reinforce the correct meaning of each word in a homophone pair. Divide your class into several small groups. Instruct each group to compose a short story that contains several homophones. Collect the completed stories and type or rewrite each one, using the incorrect choice for several of the homophones. Duplicate a class supply of each story and distribute a copy of each one to every student. Instruct your class to circle the incorrect homophone choices. Review the corrected stories for added reinforcement.

One Hundred Homophones

How many homophones can your students name? Initiate a challenge for them to think of 100 homophone pairs. Post a sheet of chart paper in an easily accessible place. Have your students brainstorm a list of homophone pairs while you record the words on the chart paper. (If desired, use a different-colored marker for each ten pairs so that counting will be easier.) If the resulting list is a few pairs short, extend the challenge for a few more days. After your goal has been reached, display the completed chart as a handy reference.

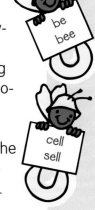

Synonyms And Antonyms

Match Game Review

Review the concept of words with the same meanings (synonyms) and words with opposite meanings (antonyms) with this matching activity. Write each word from several synonym (or antonym) pairs on the chalkboard in random order. Select a student to come to the board and circle two of the words that create a synonym (or antonym) pair. To check her work, the student asks the class for a thumbs-up or thumbs-down sign. If her answer is correct, the student calls a new player to the board. If the answer is incorrect, she erases the circles before calling the next player.

angry	dirty	correct
cry	below	road
right	jump	leap
street	clean	mad
bad	win	above
lose	weep	good

Cookie Jar Sorting

This mouthwatering activity will provide students with a tasty way to review synonyms and antonyms. To prepare, obtain two small cookie jars. Label one jar "synonyms" and the other "antonyms." Place the jars in a learning center along with a supply of cookie-shaped cutouts. When a student thinks of a pair of synonyms or antonyms, he writes them on a cutout and stores it in the appropriate jar. Review the contents of each jar with the class at the end of every week.

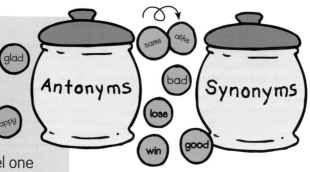

Word Skill Activities

Use the words lists and patterns on the following pages (pp. 49-55) to help students practice an assortment of word skills. See the examples for ideas, or use your imagination to make materials for learning-center activities, partner reviews, and individual reinforcement practice.

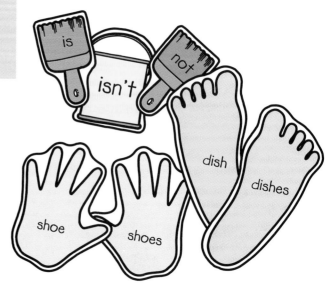

48

Prefixes And Suffixes

Prefixes

A prefix is a letter or sequence of letters attached to the beginning of a word, root, or phrase to change its meaning.

Prefix	Meaning	Prefix	Meaning
ante-	before	mid-	middle
anti-	against	mis-	wrong
bi-	two, twice	mono-	one, single
co-	together	non-	not
counter-	against	out-	greater, better
de-	opposite of, remove from, reduce	over-	beyond, too much
dis-	not, do the opposite of	post-	after
en-	made of, belonging to, consisting of	pre-	before, in front of
		re-	again
ex-	out	sub-	under, part of a whole
fore-	in front of	tele-	far away
hyper-	more than usual	trans-	move from one place to another, across
hypo-	under		
im-, in-, ir-	not	tri-	three
inter-	between	un-	not, opposite of

Suffixes

A suffix is a letter or sequence of letters that may be added to the end of a word, root, or phrase to change its meaning.

Suffix	Meaning	Suffix	Meaning
-able, -ible	able to, capable of	-ics	study of, act or practice of
-al	belonging to, process of action, relating to	-ion	result of an act or process
		-ish	nationality, having likeness to
-ance, -ence, -ancy, -ency	quality, act, or condition	-ive	having the quality of, tending to
-ant	to be or perform in a certain way	-less	without
		-let	smallness in size, worn on the body
-ar	of or relating to, being	-like	similar to
-ate	result or act of	-ly	in a certain manner
-dom	area ruled by, condition or state of being	-ment	result of, action or process
		-ness	manner or state of being
-er	person or thing belonging to or associated with, one that does or performs	-or	one who does something, state or act
		-ship	state of, office or skill
-er, -est	superlative adjective	-tion, -sion	state of doing something
-ful	full of	-ty, -ity	state, quality, or amount
-fy	to form into or become	-ward	toward, in the direction of
-hood	state of being, membership in a group	-wise	in position of, with regard to
		-y, -ey	quality or state of
-ic	like, pertaining to		

Contractions

A contraction is a shortened form of single word or a word pair. An apostrophe is used to show where a letter or letters have been omitted to create the shortened form.

words with "am"

I am	I'm

words with "are"

they are	they're
we are	we're
you are	you're

words with "has"

he has	he's
it has	it's
she has	she's
what has	what's
where has	where's
who has	who's

words with "have"

I have	I've
they have	they've
you have	you've
we have	we've

words with "is"

he is	he's
it is	it's
she is	she's
that is	that's
there is	there's
what is	what's
where is	where's
who is	who's

words with "not"

are not	aren't
cannot	can't
could not	couldn't
did not	didn't
do not	don't
does not	doesn't
had not	hadn't
have not	haven't
has not	hasn't
is not	isn't
must not	mustn't
should not	shouldn't
was not	wasn't
were not	weren't
will not	won't
would not	wouldn't

words with "us"

let us	let's

words with "will"

he will	he'll
I will	I'll
she will	she'll
they will	they'll
we will	we'll
you will	you'll

words with "would"

he would	he'd
I would	I'd
she would	she'd
they would	they'd
who would	who'd
you would	you'd

Compound Words

afternoon	chalkboard	fingernail	hopscotch	outline	snowball	toothache
airline	clothespin	firecracker	horseback	outside	snowflake	toothbrush
airplane	cobweb	firefighter	horsefly	overall	snowman	treetop
anybody	copycat	firefly	horseshoe	overcome	somebody	underground
anyone	cornbread	fireman	hourglass	overlook	someday	underline
anything	corncob	fireplace	houseboat	overtime	someone	understand
anyway	cornmeal	firewood	household	paintbrush	something	underwear
anywhere	cowboy	fireworks	housewife	pancake	somewhere	upright
armchair	cowgirl	fishbowl	hubcap	patchwork	spaceship	wallpaper
arrowhead	cupboard	fisherman	indoor	peanut	springtime	warehouse
artwork	cupcake	flagpole	inside	pillowcase	stagecoach	washcloth
ballpark	daybreak	flashlight	into	pincushion	stairway	watchman
bareback	daydream	flowerpot	junkyard	playground	starfish	waterfall
barnyard	daylight	football	keyboard	pocketbook	starlight	watermelon
baseball	doghouse	footprint	ladybug	policeman	steamroller	weekend
basketball	dollhouse	friendship	landmark	popcorn	stopwatch	whatever
bathrobe	doorbell	gentleman	landowner	postman	storeroom	wheelbarrow
bathroom	doorknob	gingerbread	lifetime	quarterback	storybook	whenever
bathtub	doormat	goldfish	lighthouse	railroad	strawberry	whirlwind
bedroom	doorway	grandfather	lookout	rainbow	suitcase	whoever
bedspread	doughnut	grandmother	lunchroom	raincoat	summertime	wildlife
bedtime	downhill	grapefruit	mailbox	raindrop	sunburn	windmill
beehive	downstairs	grasshopper	mailman	rattlesnake	Sunday	windshield
birdbath	downtown	greenhouse	mealtime	roadside	sundown	wintertime
birdhouse	driftwood	groundhog	milkman	rowboat	sunflower	within
birthday	driveway	grownup	milkshake	runway	sunlight	without
blackboard	drugstore	hairbrush	moonbeam	sailboat	sunrise	woodland
blacksmith	drumstick	haircut	moonlight	salesman	sunset	worthwhile
bluebird	eardrum	halfway	moonstone	sandpaper	sunshine	yourself
boxcar	earring	handshake	motorboat	scarecrow	sweatband	
breakfast	earthquake	headache	motorcycle	schoolhouse	sweatshirt	
broomstick	eggplant	headband	mousetrap	schoolyard	sweetheart	
buckskin	eggshell	headfirst	necklace	scrapbook	swordfish	
butterball	evergreen	headlight	necktie	seahorse	tablecloth	
buttercup	everybody	headline	newspaper	seashell	tablespoon	
butterfly	everyone	headrest	nightcap	seashore	taillight	
campfire	everything	headstand	nighttime	seesaw	teacup	
campground	everywhere	headstrong	nobody	shipwreck	teamwork	
cardboard	eyeball	heatstroke	notebook	shoebox	teapot	
cannot	eyebrow	highchair	nothing	sidewalk	teaspoon	
catbird	eyelash	hillside	outcome	situp	textbook	
catfish	eyelid	homemade	outdoors	skateboard	thumbtack	
cattail	farmland	homework	outhouse	smokestack	toadstool	

Homophones, Synonyms, Antonyms

Homophones

ate-eight	course-coarse	hair-hare	loan-lone	pray-prey	tacks-tax
be-bee	creak-creek	haul-hall	made-maid	red-read	tail-tale
bear-bare	deer-dear	hear-here	male-mail	road-rode	there-their
beet-beat	do-dew	him-hymn	meat-meet	sale-sail	through-threw
blew-blue	eye-I	hole-whole	none-nun	sea-see	to-too-two
bored-board	fair-fare	hour-our	oh-owe	sew-so	wait-weight
break-brake	feat-feet	knead-need	one-won	sight-site	waste-waist
buy-by-bye	flour-flower	knew-new-gnu	pail-pale	soar-sore	way-weigh
carrot-caret	forth-fourth	knight-night	pair-pear	some-sum	week-weak
cell-sell	fur-fir	knot-not	pane-pain	son-sun	would-wood
cents-scents-sense	great-grate	know-no	piece-peace	stare-stair	write-right
	groan-grown	knows-nose	plane-plain	steak-stake	

Synonyms

above-over	considerate-kind	enemy-foe	grin-smile	look-see	soggy-wet
afraid-scared	correct-right	false-untrue	hard-difficult	loud-noisy	story-tale
alike-same	cry-weep	fast-quick	healthy-well	many-several	stroll-walk
angry-mad	damage-destroy	fight-quarrel	home-house	neat-tidy	surprised-startled
auto-car	different-varied	find-discover	incorrect-wrong	odd-strange	throw-toss
begin-start	dirty-filthy	fix-repair	intelligent-smart	rip-tear	
below-under	drink-beverage	friend-pal	jog-run	road-street	
big-large	drowsy-sleepy	funny-humorous	jump-leap	shout-yell	
buy-purchase	easy-simple	glad-happy	keep-save	skinny-thin	
chilly-cold	end-finish	go-leave	late-tardy	small-tiny	

Antonyms

above-below	buy-sell	destroy-repair	float-sink	loose-tight	right-wrong
add-subtract	catch-throw	difficult-easy	forget-remember	lose-win	rough-smooth
alike-different	clean-dirty	down-up	found-lost	mean-nice	save-spend
asleep-awake	close-open	dry-wet	frown-smile	narrow-wide	short-tall
backward-forward	cold-hot	early-late	generous-selfish	noisy-quiet	sour-sweet
bad-good	come-go	enemy-friend	give-take	old-new	tame-wild
beautiful-ugly	crooked-straight	false-true	happy-sad	over-under	terrible-wonderful
begin-finish	cry-laugh	fancy-plain	hard-soft	peace-war	whisper-yell
believe-doubt	dangerous-safe	fast-slow	healthy-sick	play-work	
big-small	day-night	fat-thin	left-right	polite-rude	
	deep-shallow	few-many		poor-rich	

Use with "Word Skill Activities" on page 48.

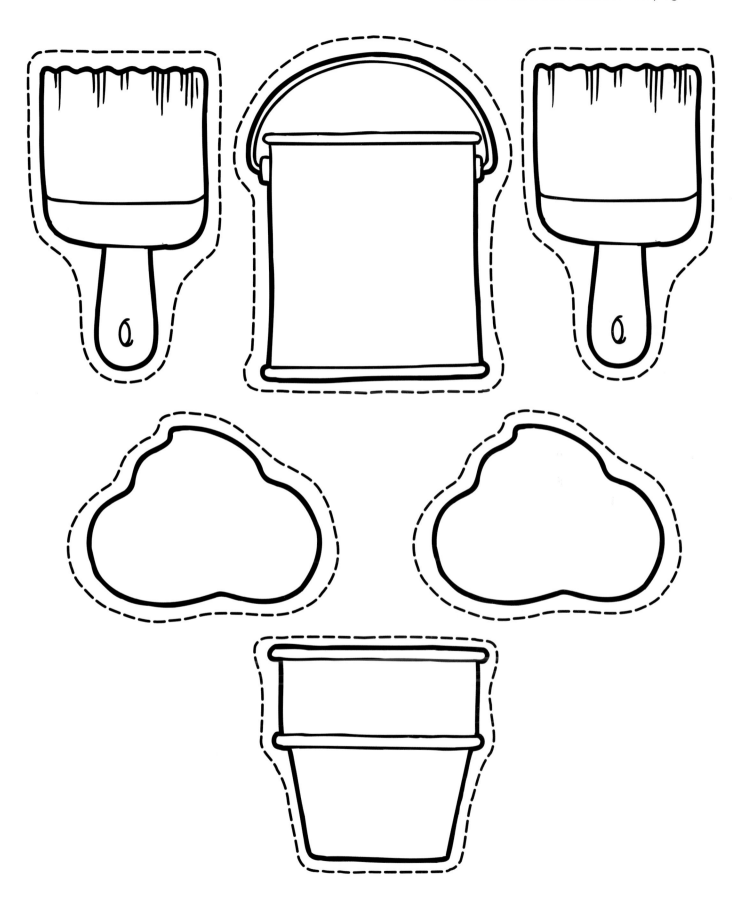

Patterns

Use with "Word Skill Activities" on page 48.

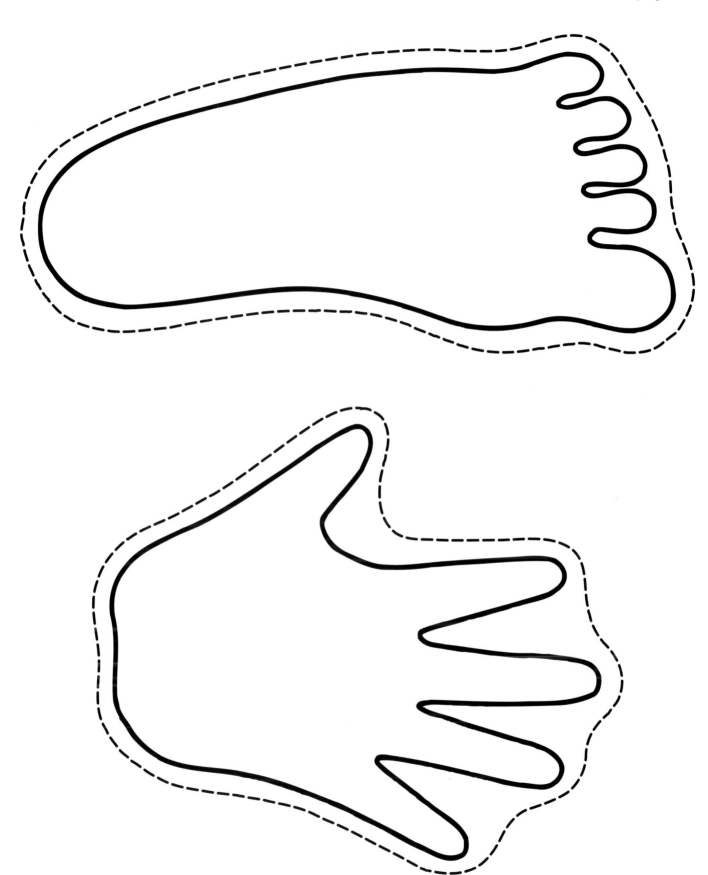

Vocabulary Enrichment

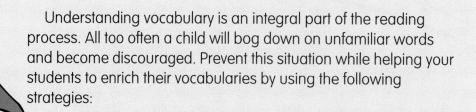

Understanding vocabulary is an integral part of the reading process. All too often a child will bog down on unfamiliar words and become discouraged. Prevent this situation while helping your students to enrich their vocabularies by using the following strategies:

- Teach students to read context instead of just words; stress the meaning of the entire sentence or passage instead of an isolated word. Model the process by writing on the chalkboard a sentence with a blank in place of one of the words. Ask students to determine possible choices for the missing word.

- Before reading with your students, make a list of possible unfamiliar words. Write them on the board, read them aloud, and define them for the class. Check for understanding by having student volunteers use the words in sentences. Then refer to each word as it appears in the story or reading material.

- Add to your students' vocabulary backgrounds by selecting read-alouds that are slightly above grade level. At the end of each chapter or passage, review new terms and reinforce the understanding of new words through context clues. Ask students which parts of the story helped them to understand the new vocabulary words.

- Take a cue from popular calendars and have a "Word Of The Day." Write a new word and its definition on the chalkboard. Offer incentives to children who can correctly use the word in their speaking or writing during the day.

- Keep a supply of children's thesauruses in your classroom. Or, if your students have access to computers, encourage them to use the thesaurus on their computers as they write. The alternative word choices will present them with new ways to state already familiar words.

Developing Vocabulary

Help your students connect vocabulary words with familiar meanings by creating prereading word banks. Prior to reading a story, write a topic on the chalkboard and have your students brainstorm a list of words that relate to the topic. A word bank for the topic *families* might look like this:

mother	kitchen	baby
father	sister	shopping
house	brother	uncle
vacation	mobile home	farm
children	pets	cousins
chores	grandparents	condominium
apartment	birthdays	camping

Have your students read aloud the words on the list and use them in sentences that tell about families. Then extend the activity by having your students divide the list into smaller categories. For example, the list above could be categorized as *People In Families, Where Families Live,* and *Things Families Do.*

This vocabulary activity works with a variety of general topics, making it ideal for introducing most children's books. Use these topic guidelines as a reference:

School (people, subjects, activities)
Holidays (what people do, how we decorate, what we eat)
Sports (what we wear, what we use, positions people play)
Community (people, jobs, transportation)
Seasons (weather, activities, what we wear)
Friends (what we play, how we act, why friends are important)
Pets (what they need, types of pets, things to do with pets)

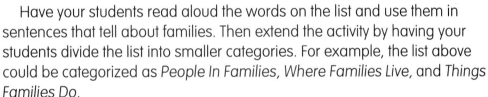

Word Of The Day

ally

giddy

hesitate

Vocabulary development can be an easy part of your morning routine. To introduce a new word each day, simply write the word and its definition on a corner of the chalkboard for students to observe as they come in each morning. Discuss the pronunciation of the word and read aloud its definition. Ask student volunteers to use the word in a sentence. If desired, make a list of different forms of the word, including prefixes, suffixes, and different tenses. Then challenge your students to use the word in oral or written work throughout the day.

The Word Of The Day can also be used with these activities:

content

- Include the week's Word Of The Day words as bonus words on your spelling test.

- At the end of the month, prepare an assessment requiring students to match the previous Word Of The Day words with their corresponding definitions.

genuine

- Assign a short daily homework assignment requiring each student to write a sentence that includes that day's featured word.

- At the end of the week, post a list of the words that have been intro-duced during the week. Challenge each student to write a story that includes all the words on the list.

distress

- Place a dictionary in a learning center and have students look up the Word Of The Day. Encourage students to find the guide words on the page, the words immediately before and after the featured word, its part of speech, its number of syllables, and its accented syllable.

bashful

Dictionary

scheme

annoy

parcel dowdy

Monthly Word Box

Kick off the beginning of each new month by starting a Monthly Word Box. To make this simple project, decorate an empty shoebox and gather a supply of index cards and a marker. On the first day of the month, ask students to share words that relate to holidays, activities, important people, and other information about the new month. Record each word on a separate index card and store it in the box. Use the word cards for group or independent learning activities. Here are a dozen ideas for using your Monthly Word Box:

- placing the words in alphabetical order
- sorting parts of speech
- identifying proper nouns
- having each student illustrate a word card
- listing rhyming words, synonyms, or antonyms
- using the words as reading flash cards
- copying words for handwriting practice
- writing sentences with predetermined words from the box
- classifying words into different categories
- counting the syllables in each word
- looking up words in the dictionary
- learning to spell designated words for a monthly spelling test

Encourage students to think of additional cards to add to the box throughout the month. At the end of the month, place the box in an accessible spot. You can refer to previous word boxes to compare the number of nouns from each month, the different holidays named, or the total number of cards made for the entire year. Refresh students' vocabulary words by reviewing cards from past months as well.

cranberry

ghost

corn

thankful

holiday

night

turkey

leaves · hool

dy

feast · kin

September

October

November

Vocabulary Enrichment

Flash-Card Fun

How do you make vocabulary reinforcement more inviting? Why not build on your students' interests to expand their vocabularies! The following flash-card activity is designed for the topic of animals and their babies, but you can adapt the idea for a variety of subjects. Determine what topic will capture your students' interest and go from there!

To begin, make a set of flash cards for the words on the list. Use the cards for your favorite flash-card games, or try the activities described at right.

Word List

bear	cub
beaver	kit
cat	kitten
chicken	chick
cow	calf
deer	fawn
dog	puppy
duck	duckling
goat	kid
goose	gosling
horse	foal
kangaroo	joey
lion	cub
pig	piglet
seal	pup
sheep	lamb
swan	cygnet
turkey	poult
whale	calf

Word Sorting

Word sorting promotes word understanding and encourages students to analyze words. Have your students work individually or in groups to sort words according to these categories:

- adult animals/baby animals
- mammals/birds
- two-legged animals/four-legged animals
- number of letters in animal names
- one-syllable words/two-syllable words
- wild animals/domesticated animals

Venn Diagrams

You can also use the flash cards to have your students create Venn diagrams. As the children analyze each card, they will develop a deeper understanding of the word as well as develop stronger word-recognition skills. Graphing skills will also be reinforced, making this activity a well-rounded one!

For a fun way for students to create Venn diagrams, purchase colorful Hula-Hoops®. Place the hoops on the floor in an overlapping fashion. Label each section of the hoops with a classification. Have your students place the word cards in the corresponding sections of the hoops.

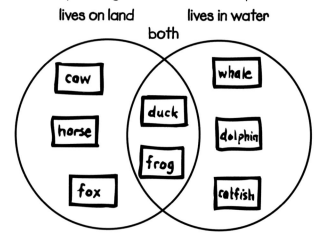

Vocabulary Enrichment

Animal Attributes

Encourage students to use critical-thinking skills as they determine similarities and differences among the animals named in your flash-card deck. To start the activity, invite your students to sit in a circle. Distribute a flash card to each child and keep one for yourself. Ask the child sitting to your left, "How is your animal like mine?" The student may respond that his animal has the same number of legs, lives in the same habitat, has similar coloring, or has the same type of protective covering. Continue around the circle until each student has had the opportunity to participate. Then turn the tables on your class by asking, "How is your animal different from mine?" Add to the challenge by having each student name two differences or by asking him to name a similarity and a difference between the animals.

Student partners can also play another version of the game. Instruct the partners to divide the deck equally, then turn their cards facedown. The students count to three and then turn over the top cards on their decks. Each student must name a similarity (or difference) between the animals before turning over the next cards in their decks. Before long your students will know all about animals!

Flash-Card Story Starters

There's no end to the stories that can be created with ideas generated from the flash-card deck. To get your students started on a story, place the flash cards facedown on a table and instruct each student to select two or three cards. Have the student use the words featured on her selected cards to create a story idea. After each student has written her story, provide time for her to share it with the class. For an added feature, have classmates in the listening audience try to identify the flash cards the writer used to develop her story. With a flash-card deck on hand, there will always be a wealth of ideas waiting!

Vocabulary Enrichment

Class Books

One of the best ways for students to build vocabulary is to use it in a meaningful project. Class booklets provide the perfect opportunity for students to use newly learned words while making something that can be enjoyed time and time again. The following ideas can be used with the flash-card vocabulary described on page 60, new subject terminology, or any other vocabulary you wish to reinforce.

Word Matchup

Students will enjoy making and reading this simple interactive book. To make the book, provide each student with a 12" x 18" sheet of white construction paper. Instruct each student to visually divide her paper in half. On each side she illustrates and labels one part of a matching pair, such as an animal and its offspring, a state and its motto or flower, or a book cover and its main character.

To assemble the book, instruct each student to fold the right side of her page in half toward the middle so that one part of the pair is hidden from view. Compile the pages into a booklet and add a construction-paper cover. Staple the left side of the booklet together and display the booklet for your class to enjoy.

Alphabet Books

Alphabet books can be a wonderful way to review any subject matter while encouraging students to stretch their vocabularies. To prepare for making an alphabet book, assign each student several letters of the alphabet and distribute a sheet of construction paper for each letter. Name a topic for the book, and instruct each student to illustrate and describe on each page something about the topic that begins with his assigned letters. Collect the completed pages and staple them between a cover labeled "The ABCs Of _____."

Vocabulary Enrichment

Antonym Adventures

Antonym pairs will provide story starters in this creative-writing project. To begin, ask your students to brainstorm a list of antonym pairs while you record their responses on the board. Instruct each student to select one word from each of ten different pairs and use her selected words in a story. After writing the story, have her underline the words she chose from the list. Then ask her to replace each underlined word with its antonym. Provide time for students to share their "Antonym Adventures" with the class; then compile the stories into a class book for independent reading time.

Synonym Stories

This class-created book provides plenty of practice with synonyms. Distribute a 9" x 12" sheet of construction paper to each student. Announce a topic for the book, such as a trip to the circus or traveling in outer space. Instruct each student to think of a synonym pair. Have the student use one word of the pair to write a sentence and create an illustration relating to the assigned topic. The student underlines the word in the sentence, then rewrites the sentence on the back of his paper using a synonym to replace the underlined word. Collect the completed papers and compile them into a book. Read the resulting story to the class, pausing after each page for students to name the synonym for the underlined word in each sentence. Turn the page to reveal the answer. Synonyms have never been so much fun!

Which Does NOT Belong?

Broaden your students' vocabularies by encouraging a little dictionary research. Explain to your class that they are going to make a word-puzzle book in which their classmates will have to determine which word in a group does not belong. To make a page for the book, each child will need a sheet of drawing paper. Instruct him to label his paper with the following question: "Which word does NOT belong?" Next have the student list three words that have a related meaning and one word that does not fit into the group. The words should not be in a particular order, and the student may wish to consult the dictionary for words that will present a challenge to his classmates. On the back of his paper, the student identifies which word does not belong and writes an explanation telling how the other words are related. Staple the completed pages between a construction-paper cover bearing the title "Which Does NOT Belong?" Encourage students to read the book during independent work time, using the dictionary if necessary to solve the question on each page.

Vocabulary Enrichment

Laugh Your Head Off!

Your students will encounter idiomatic expressions sprinkled throughout both written and spoken language. Idioms can be wonderful vocabulary-enriching tools as students are made aware of both the figurative and literal meanings behind them. Share the idioms listed below with your students and discuss each one. Then extend the lesson into a bookmaking project as each student selects an idiom to explain and illustrate on a copy of the reproducible on page 65. Students will get a chuckle as they see how the literal meaning creates a very different picture from the figurative message. Compile the completed pages into a class booklet titled "We're Laughing Our Heads Off!" Continue tickling funny bones by having each student take home the book to share with his family overnight.

Idiomatic Expressions

two peas in a pod	raining cats and dogs
button your lip	walking on air
off your rocker	turn over a new leaf
having a green thumb	in the same boat
keep a stiff upper lip	by the skin of your teeth
let the cat out of the bag	knock me over with a feather
seeing eye to eye	put your foot in your mouth
'til the cows come home	stop on a dime
in hot water	that's the way the cookie crumbles
full of baloney	straight from the horse's mouth
head over heels	over the hill
burning your bridges	by the seat of his pants
on pins and needles	lend a hand
pulling my leg	in the same boat
trying to catch your eye	laugh your head off

Laugh Your Head Off!

Have you ever heard of this idiom?

_____

This is what it means:

_____

_____

But this is what it looks like!

Note To Teacher: Use with "Laugh Your Head Off!" on page 64.

Reading Comprehension

Reading comprehension is the litmus test of how well children can read. Many young students learn to read aloud quite impressively but retain little of what has been read. By helping students comprehend what they read you are promoting:

- the connection between the written word and the real world
- the skills necessary for success in school and work endeavors
- avid, not reluctant, readers
- self-confidence and self-esteem
- analytical skills
- lifelong readers
- the key to understanding in all subject matters

Children in the second and third grades should already have the ability to understand both oral and written materials. They should be able to listen to and understand the content and details of a selection read aloud to them. In addition, they should be able to read a selection and demonstrate the following skills:

- sequencing events
- drawing conclusions
- determining main idea
- making inferences
- retelling the selection
- recalling details
- identifying the characters, plot, and setting of a story

There are many ways to evaluate the progress of your students. Both written and oral assessments are useful in determining the ability level of each child. This section will provide you with ideas for helping students make gains in reading comprehension to ensure future success as confident readers.

The Role Of The Teacher

Teachers are often hard-pressed to conjure up yet one more way to increase comprehension skills in their classrooms. A typical class might consist of a few students who seem to have been born reading, as well as those who seem to say, "Teach me if you dare!" Having a variety of ability levels in your room can actually benefit everyone. While you plan activities to reach the different learners in your classroom, you will undoubtedly find a certain activity or teaching style that reaches a student who has been so far unresponsive. Remember that reading comprehension should be a positive, nonthreatening process and should be approached by instilling a love of, not a fear of, reading.

High-Frequency Words

Help your students gain more from reading by making sure they are familiar with these high-frequency words. Refer to the sections on phonics games (pages 30–33) as well as word wall activities (pages 34–41) for ideas on how to present the words.

about	forty	once	though
again	fourth	party	thought
along	friend	people	through
always	goes	piece	too
aunt	guess	please	trouble
because	half	pretty	two
before	have	ready	until
blue	hear	receive	use
built	heard	remember	vacation
busy	here	right	very
buy	hour	rough	were
children	instead	said	we're
come	knew	school	when
coming	know	several	where
could	lessons	since	which
country	letter	special	white
cousin	little	straight	whole
does	making	suppose	women
early	many	surprise	would
easy	minute	teacher	write
enough	nice	tear	writing
every	none	their	wrote
favorite	off	there	your
first	often	they	you're

Comprehension Activities

Up And Down

This activity will reinforce story details and provide your students with a visual map of story plotting. Best of all, you'll find that this activity can be adapted to any story. To introduce the concept of story plotting to your students, use a familiar tale such as "Cinderella" to model the procedure. Refer to the example below to guide your students in plotting the ups and downs of this fairy-tale character.

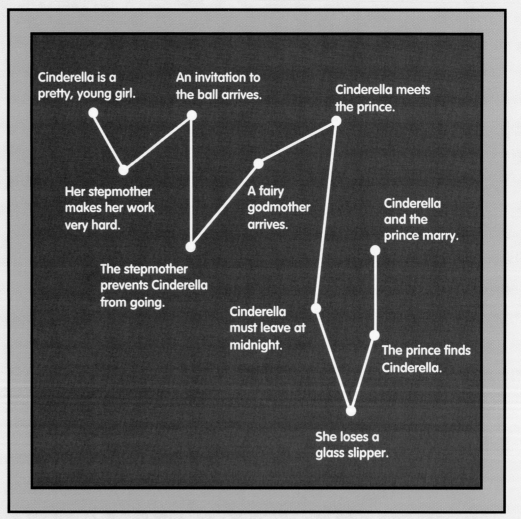

Cinderella is a pretty, young girl.

An invitation to the ball arrives.

Cinderella meets the prince.

Her stepmother makes her work very hard.

A fairy godmother arrives.

Cinderella and the prince marry.

The stepmother prevents Cinderella from going.

Cinderella must leave at midnight.

The prince finds Cinderella.

She loses a glass slipper.

Extend the activity to review story sequence. Write each of the story details on different tagboard sentence strips. Distribute the strips to student partners and have the class work together to sequence the events as they occurred in the story.

Getting The Picture

Create a visual way for students to get the "big picture" of a story or reading selection. After students have finished reading, distribute a sheet of drawing paper to each child. Instruct her to fold her paper into fourths, then unfold and number each section of the paper. Instruct each student to think of four important events from the reading selection and draw them in sequential order on her paper. Provide time for each student to show her completed work to the class. After all papers have been shared, have the class review the important story details while you record the answers on the chalkboard. Have the students help you number each detail in order. The important events and the sequence will be reinforced, helping students to comprehend the main ideas of the reading selection.

Prereading Predictions

Don't overlook prediction skills when it comes to reading comprehension. Prior to reading a selection with your class, create a list of important vocabulary words from the story. Include people, places, events, objects, and descriptions that are important to the story. Display the list and have students use the words as clues to predict possible characters, plots, and settings. Record students' predictions; then read the story together. Afterwards, refer to the predictions and compare them to the actual characters and events in the story. Conclude the lesson by having students each write a summary paragraph using vocabulary from the list. Sometimes a little prior knowledge goes a long way towards comprehension!

Summarized Stories

Reinforce comprehension as students summarize a chapter book they have read together (or one that you have read aloud to them). Create a group for every chapter in the book and place an equal number of students in each group. Instruct each group to review its chapter and write a paragraph summarizing (in five sentences or less) the important events. Instruct the group to add an illustration to its summary. Compile the resulting pages into a book and ask a student volunteer to design a cover. Have the groups take turns sharing the book to strengthen comprehension skills.

Prereading List

godmother   ball
stepmother   coach
slipper
charming
magic
palace

Sequencing Skills

Strengthen your students' reading skills as they sequence story events. The following activities will help students learn to recognize order of story details, adding to their overall comprehension of a reading selection.

Sequencing Strips

For a quick, hands-on sequencing activity, simply gather a supply of sentence strips and a marker. After your students read a selection together, write several of the story's events each on a separate sentence strip. (Keep the number of sentences to five or six to keep it simple and provide for quick success.) Display the completed strips on the chalk ledge (or another easy-viewing area), placing them in random order. Ask a student volunteer to identify the sentence that tells about the first event in the story. Have her place the strip in front of all the others. Continue calling on volunteers until all events are correctly sequenced. Or, for a variation on the activity, make several sets of sentence strips and have small groups work together to determine the correct sequence of the story.

Red Riding Hood went into the woods.

The wolf got in Grandmother's bed.

Red Riding Hood met the wolf.

First, Next, Last

Show students how to transfer the sequenced story events described above into a writing activity that reinforces summarization. Display the correctly sequenced sentence strips for students to observe. Instruct each student to copy the events in order, using transition words such as *first*, *second*, *next*, *then*, and *last* to show the sequence of events. The result will be a paragraph that highlights important details, sequences events, and portrays a well-developed summary of the story.

Sequencing Skills

Order, Please!

Students will be eager to put sequencing skills to use when the end result is a tasty treat! Decide on an easy-to-make snack for your students, such as peanut-butter crackers, jelly sandwiches, or celery spread with cream cheese. Tell each student that before he can make his treat, he must list in order the steps for making it. After each child has completed his sequenced list, ask for students to dictate the steps while you write them on the chalkboard. Allow for discussion as the directions are dictated; some students may want to rearrange or add steps when they see them written on the chalkboard. Review the finished directions with your students. Ask students to check for basic steps: Do the directions state to wash hands first? Is there a step for gathering materials? Is it clear how to apply the jelly (or other ingredient) on the cracker? Do the directions tell how to clean up afterwards? After pointing out these and other necessary steps, have each student revise his list. When a student shows you his newly corrected list, allow him to prepare the snack according to his directions.

> 1. **Wash hands.**
> 2. **Gather bread, jelly, and a knife.**
> 3. **Open the jelly.**
> 4. **Scoop jelly out with knife.**
> 5. **Spread jelly on bread.**
> 6. **Eat the snack.**
> 7. **Clean up.**

For a variation on the activity described above, substitute an art project for the snack. Write the directions for completing the project on separate sentence strips. Have students work together to place the directions in the correct order. After each student finishes her art project, have her name the sequenced steps she performed to complete the activity.

Say It, Sequence It

Don't forget that sequencing can be reinforced through listening skills. Test your students' auditory reaction to a list of illogically sequenced directions such as, "Sit down, close your book, read the story on page 39, and then get out your reading book." The initial reactions may include looks of confusion, giggles, or waves of hands from students eager to correct you. Ask a student to restate the directions in a logical sequence. Repeat the activity periodically to keep your students all ears.

Sequencing Skills

Sequencing Scavenger Hunt

Scavenger hunts are popular with students, and they can be a great way to reinforce sequencing skills. To prepare for a classroom scavenger hunt, develop a set of questions relating to a story. Then write each question and answer on a separate index card. Sample questions and answers for the story *Charlotte's Web* are shown below.

Questions	Answers
Who saved Wilbur when he was first born?	Fern
Who wanted to be Wilbur's friend?	Charlotte
What was Charlotte's first message?	Some Pig
What did Templeton hide that later got broken?	a rotten egg
What did Lurvy make for Wilbur?	a crate
Where did the Zuckermans take Wilbur?	to the fair
What did Fern ride with Henry Fussy?	the Ferris wheel
What was Charlotte's magnum opus?	her egg sack
How many baby spiders stayed in the barn with Wilbur?	three

Position the answer cards in various places (but in plain sight) throughout the classroom. Distribute a question to each student pair and have the pair discuss the correct answer before searching for the corresponding answer card. After all partners have located their answer cards, have the class work together to arrange the events referred to in the questions in the proper sequence. Students will enjoy "hunting" for answers with this activity that also reviews vocabulary and comprehension skills.

Sequencing Skills

Sequenced Picture Cards

Have students sharpen their sequencing skills as they record important events from a story. After reading a story together, place students in groups of four or five. Distribute crayons and an index card or a sheet of drawing paper to each member in the group. Instruct each group to write and illustrate sentences detailing events from the story. Call on each group to share its completed sentences with the class by placing the illustrations on the chalk rail in random order. When a group has shared its work, ask the class to help you arrange the pictures and sentences in the correct sequence. The completed projects can be compiled into booklets that summarize the story.

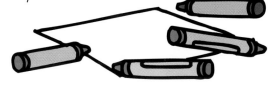

Act It Out

Encourage your students to put a touch of dramatics into this sequencing activity. Place your students in small groups and instruct each group to read a short story together. After reading, have the group members decide how to briefly act out the story for the class. Suggest that each student take the role of a different character or tell an important event from the story. Remind each group to rehearse its presentation to ensure that all events are presented in the correct order. Provide time for each group to take a turn in the spotlight as it performs a sequenced account of its story. Then invite all your performers to take a bow, and treat them to a round of applause!

Silly Sequencing

Add a chuckle to a lesson on sequencing with a little help from the funny papers. To prepare, cut out several comic strips from a newspaper. White-out the words in the speech bubbles and photocopy a class supply. Distribute a copy to each student and instruct her to use the comic strip pictures as clues in determining a sequence of events. Then have the student fill in her speech bubbles with text that shows a sequenced idea. Share the completed creations by posting the projects on a bulletin board or featuring them in your classroom newspaper.

Retelling A Story

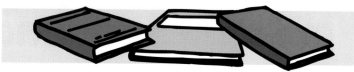

Retelling Skills

Having a student retell a story is a good way to assess if he understands the main ideas. A successful retelling should include major characters, plot details, correctly sequenced events, and the appropriate conclusion. In addition to being an important reading comprehension skill, retelling a story is also an excellent way to reinforce your students' speaking and writing skills.

Tell Me A Story

Picture books can be a great tool in promoting retelling. Read a short but eventful story to your class and model the procedure for retelling by prompting students with such questions as "Who were the important characters in the story? Where did it take place? What happened first? Then what happened? What did the character(s) do? How did the story end?" Steer students away from minor details that bog down the retelling. Stress the importance of presenting the story's highlights in a correctly sequenced order. Then encourage student volunteers to retell stories from their library books or host an oral book reporting program that will allow students to practice this skill.

Retelling A Wordless Story

Challenge your students' retelling skills with the help of wordless books. This will prove a little more difficult for some children since there are no words or names to prompt the events from the story. If possible, obtain several copies of a wordless book and distribute a copy to students placed with partners or in small groups. Provide time for students to peruse the books; then have them work together to restate the events of the story. Circulate throughout the groups to make sure that the students are on the right track. Then repeat the activity, having your students work individually to retell the story orally or in writing. Let your students decide if a picture is really worth a thousand words!

Jack traded his cow for some magic beans. Boy, was his mother mad!

Retelling A Story

Story-Go-Round

This retelling activity requires little preparation and will soon become a student favorite! All you need to get started is a large sheet of chart paper, a marker, and a place on a wall or table. (Be sure the marker will not bleed through the paper.) Before posting the chart paper, write a story starter at the top of the page. Invite children to add to the story throughout the day, but to ensure continuity, caution them to read through the entire story before adding to it. You might also wish to impose a two-sentence limit so that all students will have an opportunity to participate. Before the end of the day, read the story aloud to the class. Afterward, ask student volunteers to retell the story in their own words. Repeat the activity once a week or have it become a regular feature on a story wall (see page 76).

You can extend each story-go-round by discussing the following aspects of the completed work. As students evaluate the story, you can reinforce important skills for them to use in future retelling and writing assignments.

✔ Who is the main character?

✔ What is the setting?

✔ What is the main plot or idea?

✔ What are some details that made the story interesting?

✔ Do all events make sense?

✔ Are the events in logical order?

✔ How does the ending relate to the beginning?

✔ What other events could have happened to help the story flow?

One day I was walking in the woods. I thought I heard a noise behind me. I turned around and couldn't believe my eyes! There was a rabbit riding a motorcycle!

Story Walls

Story Walls

A story wall is a wonderful place to post your students' retellings. You can display individual works from short stories or group efforts at chapter summarization. The wall is not only a good place to show off student work, but it can also be used to help new students or children who have been absent to catch up with what the rest of the class has been reading.

Wall Walk

Your story wall can become a very useful classroom tool. The wall will be in a constant state of change as you add, delete, and edit the material posted there. Before you remove projects from the wall, however, have your students revisit the material. Ask your students to voice positive comments about the works. Have them point out which papers show good paragraph usage, which feature correct capitalization, and which have proper utilization of punctuation. Then have the class decide what to do with the papers being removed: should they be compiled into a class book, sent home with individual students, moved to a hallway display, or placed in portfolios? You might even want to place some works in a story wall museum that can be displayed during Open House or other special events.

Story Wall Box

Promote new vocabulary as students work on retelling skills. Affix a box (or envelope) to your story wall. Invite your students to place word cards that feature interesting names or words from retold stories in the box. At the end of the week, gather your students by the wall as you display the words that have been placed in the box. Encourage students to comment on the words and discuss the meanings of unfamiliar terms.

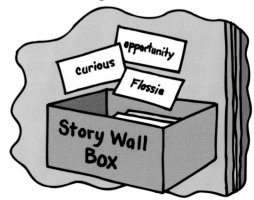

Story Walls

Other Ways To Use Story Walls

Personal Stories

There's no better background for students to use for retelling than tales from their personal lives. Students are eager to share stories of vacations, holidays, new babies, pets, and a host of other topics. Ask each student to retell in writing a favorite family tale. To add to the personalized touch, invite students to decorate their stories with photos, magazine cutouts, or drawings. Post the stories on the story wall for all classmates to enjoy.

Last year we went to the beach. I looked for shells. I also went swimming. I love the ocean.

Erroneous Retellings

Invite your students to participate in altered story retellings in which classmates try to uncover incorrect story details. Have each student select a library book to use for a written retelling exercise. In the retelling, however, the student should add a detail that doesn't actually occur in the story. Post the "erroneous retellings" on the story wall for students to read and research. Which supersleuths can locate the fallacious facts?

The Week In Review

Use your story wall as a place for students to reflect on the week in review. At the end of each week, have students refer to their journals or brainstorm events that have occurred at school or in the news. Make a brief list on the chalkboard of the topics students recall. Then initiate a retelling assignment in which each student writes a summary of the past week. Remind students to write about the events in the order in which they occurred. Post the completed works on the story wall. If desired, include several weekly reviews in your classroom newsletter.

This week was a fun week. We read a book about frogs. We watched a film about toads. Then we made tadpoles out of clay.

Recalling Details

While we spend considerable time and energy helping students locate main ideas, the supporting details are equally important. The details often help students make inferences, make predictions, and find the main ideas. The details also add to the overall understanding of a passage. You can help students pay attention to detail as you point out specific items in books you read aloud to the class. There are also game-type activities that can enhance attention to detail. Try the following suggestions with your students and watch as they find all the parts that make up the sum of the whole.

Details, Details

Help students pay attention to detail with a tried-and-true favorite activity—show-and-tell! Students are always eager to share stories and show treasured objects to the class, and you can capitalize on their enthusiasm by asking them to include details in their presentations. Model a detailed presentation by introducing an object of your own to the class. As you show the object, explain the significance of the item and announce, "This is a special object to me because…and three details I would like to tell you about are…" Students will soon catch on that the details add a great deal to the total picture.

Describe It!

Challenge your students to recall details with this activity that capitalizes description. Select a familiar classroom object and direct your students' attention to it. After one minute, remove the object or hide it from view. Challenge each student to list ten details about the object. If necessary, prompt your class with questions such as, *What colors did you see? What shapes did you notice? Was there anything broken or damaged? Was there another object by it? Was there writing or markings on it? Did it have movable parts? Did it have an odor or a fragrance?* After a designated time period, allow students to share their details with the class.

Word Associations

This memory game will help your students focus on descriptive detail. To prepare for the activity, list ten nouns on the chalkboard. Ask student volunteers to name adjectives to describe each noun. Record their answers on the board; then review the list with the class. Tell the students to visualize each object as they read the words on the board. Next have your students close their eyes while you erase the adjectives from the list. Instruct students to open their eyes, study the list, and try to recall the missing adjective for each noun. Have students respond orally, or, if desired, have them write the adjectives from memory. Repeat the activity several times a week to help your students reflect on describing details. You can also incorporate a vocabulary review as you pull from words that have recently been introduced to your students.

What's The Big Idea?

Show students how important supporting details can be with this project that focuses on both details and main ideas. To begin, choose an object that interests students or that correlates with a current topic of study. Display a picture of the desired item and write a topic sentence about it on the chalkboard or on a sheet of chart paper. Next have students supply details that relate to the picture and sentence. If dinosaurs have your class in a dither, use one of the creatures for a topic. Start off with a topic sentence such as, "The tyrannosaurus was a meat eater." Your students will be eager to supply details such as, "It had very sharp teeth," or "It ran after its prey on two legs." After a desired number of details have been added, review the topic sentence and point out how all other sentences supply additional information about it. After you model a few more examples, your students will be anxious to try the activity on their own!

Main Idea

Main Idea

The main idea of a paragraph is often the topic sentence, so it is essential to reinforce both concepts to students. Understanding the main idea of a reading selection will enable students to retain more information about what they are reading. It will also help them to write fluent paragraphs and to locate information efficiently. The following activities are designed to help students zero in on main idea and topic sentences through reading and writing projects.

What's The Big Deal?

Recognizing the main idea will help students understand plot developments. Help students locate the main idea by explaining that it is the most important thing that the author is saying, or the "big deal" about the story or reading selection. Many times, the main idea is the first sentence in a paragraph, but it can also be found elsewhere in the paragraph. Provide your students with short, simple paragraphs at first and have them identify which sentence holds the main idea. Point out how other sentences give additional information about the topic but do not tell the "big deal." After additional practice, your students will easily recognize that finding the main idea IS a big deal!

Share The Main Idea

A classroom sharing time can help reinforce main-idea skills. Ask each student to bring from home an item she would like to show to the class. In advance, each student must prepare a short paragraph about the object, making sure to include a main idea as well as additional details. When the student shows her object and reads her paragraph, she concludes her presentation by asking, "What is my main idea?" She then calls on student volunteers to answer the question. The student who correctly identifies the main idea is the next to make a presentation.

This is my favorite doll. I got her for Christmas. I named her Charlotte. She sleeps with me at night. I always take good care of her.

Main Idea

Build Around The Main Idea

Help your students learn about main idea from the inside out. Post a topic sentence on the board for each student to build into a paragraph with supporting details. To model the process, use a simple topic sentence such as "My dog is very playful." Discuss the sentence and ask students to supply details that reinforce the main idea. Examples might include details about the dog chasing balls, burying bones, chasing its tail, or playing tug with an old rope. Redirect details that stray from the topic, such as the dog likes to eat cookies, doesn't like its bath, or sleeps by the front door. Once students understand that all supporting sentences must relate to the main idea, they will be ready to write paragraphs independently. Try this activity once a week to help reinforce the main idea in both reading and writing.

> My dog is very playful.
> He runs in circles.
> He chases after balls.
> He likes to go for walks.
> My dog likes to play.

Fun And Games With Main Idea

Add a little fun and games to your lesson on main idea by having students relate the concept to their favorite games. If possible, have students examine the directions for a game of checkers, Candyland®, or other familiar games. Point out that the stated object for the game is like the main idea—it tells what the game is all about. All the rules and steps listed for play are the supporting details that reinforce the object of the game. Next have each student think of a favorite game to use in a writing assignment. Have him begin the paragraph with a topic sentence that states the object of the game. Then have him complete the paragraph by describing the steps and rules for the game. Remind him to keep the steps in sequence so that the directions are easy to understand. Finally, provide time for students to read their paragraphs aloud for classmates to constructively critique.

Making Inferences

Learning to make inferences gives students the power to read between the lines and develop a deeper understanding of the story. So often, an unstated message is an important one. Teach students to look for implied meanings in the way characters speak, the clothes they wear, and their body language. When students see the big picture, a deeper level of comprehension will take place.

Rhyme And Reason

Use familiar rhymes and stories to convey the idea of inferences to your class. Start out, for example, with the nursery rhyme about Jack and Jill. Write on the chalkboard the lines "Jack and Jill went up the hill to fetch a pail of water. Jack fell down and broke his crown and Jill came tumbling after." Ask students to read the rhyme aloud with you, then think about all the information that can be deduced from the two lines. Ask questions such as:

- Can we assume that Jack and Jill were carrying something?
- What was at the top of the hill?
- Was it a steep hill?
- Did they succeed in getting water?
- Do you think they were climbing together or going one at a time?

As students volunteer answers, ask them to point out the words that implied the answers to the questions. Then, for further practice, write another nursery rhyme, such as "Little Miss Muffet" or "Old King Cole," on the board and challenge each student to list five inferences that can be made about the rhyme.

Inference Gifts

Most students have experienced the excitement of giving or receiving presents. Giving a storybook character a present can also be lots of fun. Ask your class to think about the different characters in a book you have read together. Tell students that they are going to infer what type of present would be best suited for one of the characters. Distribute a six-inch square of white construction paper to each student. Instruct him to decorate the front to make it look like a wrapped package for one of the characters, with a labeled gift tag included. Have him illustrate what is inside the package on the back of the square and include a sentence telling why it is an appropriate gift for the character. Provide time for students to share the completed works with their classmates.

To: King Cole

Old King Cole would get a pipe because he called for it.

Making Inferences

Guess What Happened!

Use stories from students' past experiences to have the class practice inferencing skills. Instruct each student to think of a story she would like to tell the class. Instruct her to leave out a detail that can be implied from the rest of the story. For example, a student may tell of a vacation in which she built a sand castle, collected shells, and learned to swim. Her classmates can infer that the vacation took place at the beach. When a classmate makes a correct inference about the story, she may take a turn sharing an experience with the class.

"What If" Inferences

Promote inference skills as you ask students to infer how story characters might react to a certain situation or resolve a problem. After reading a book together, discuss how the characters responded to certain events in the story. Then have students use what they know about the characters to decide how each one might react to the situations listed below. Have each student select a situation and a character and then write a paragraph telling how the character would probably respond.

What might the character do...

- if he found a wallet on the street?
- if his best friend spent the night with another friend?
- if he were taking a test and saw another player cheating?
- if he broke a neighbor's window?
- if he didn't get what he wanted for Christmas?
- if he lost his lunch money?
- if he left his homework outside in the rain?
- if he missed the bus?
- if he wanted to apologize for something he had done?

Character Closets

Have students use their inferencing skills as they take a pretend peek into a storybook character's closet. Ask students to each select a character from a story you have read together or from their independent reading. Remind students to consider the likes and dislikes of the character in determining what might be in his closet. Distribute a sheet of drawing paper to each student and have him sketch an open closet. Instruct the student to fill the closet with drawings or magazine cutouts showing items that the character might keep in there. Set aside a special time for each student to present his closet collage to the class.

Drawing Conclusions

Making conclusions about what is likely to happen in a story is a skill that will help students become more analytical. It can also heighten your students' interest in stories as they become eager to find out if their predictions are correct. These activities for helping students learn to make conclusions will work with picture books, chapter books, and many other forms of literature.

Elementary, My Dear Watson!

Approach this lesson on drawing conclusions as if it were a mystery to be solved. Prepare a short scenario in which the ending has been left off. Write the scenario on the board for students to read silently. After an appropriate time period, ask students to use details from the story to think of a logical ending. Have student volunteers share their endings and explain what details prompted them to come to their conclusions.

Here are two scenarios to get you started.

- Grant saw his wallet lying on the floor in the hallway. As he bent over to pick it up, he was surprised to see the wallet move away from him. He bent down for a closer look and the wallet moved again! Then Grant heard giggling from behind the corner. Suddenly he knew what was going on!

- Pablo was late for school. His teacher had warned him not to be late again. He knew he should have hurried faster, but today he had to take extra care with his appearance. He had put on his best shirt and carefully combed his hair. Then he had ridden his bike cautiously so he wouldn't get his clothes dirty. Pablo took a deep breath as he reached the classroom door. But when he opened the door, no one was there. Then he realized...

Oh no! Today is Saturday!

Draw Your Own Conclusions

This writing project will result in a learning-center activity that everyone can enjoy. Distribute a sheet of writing paper to each student and instruct him to crease it so that a few of the bottom lines are folded behind the paper. Next have him write a short story about six to ten sentences long with the last sentence of the story omitted. The final sentence should be written on the section of the paper folded behind the page. Collect the completed stories and staple them together along the top so that the bottom sections can still be unfolded. Place the resulting booklet in a learning center. Invite students to read the book during free time, trying to conclude each ending sentence before unfolding the page to reveal the answer.

Drawing The Wrong Conclusion

When your students become proficient at drawing conclusions, put their skills to the test! Compose a story in which the ending just doesn't quite add up. (See the example.) Post the story on your story wall and invite students to rewrite the story so that the conclusion makes sense, or copy the story and write a new conclusion.

Eric couldn't wait to get outside. It was the first day of snow, and he was ready to build a snowman. He hurriedly put on his boots, coat, mittens, and hat and raced to the door. "Oops!" he cried. "I can't forget these!" He scooped up a carrot, two lumps of coal, some buttons, and an old straw hat. Once outside he hummed merrily as he rolled three large balls of snow. He worked carefully to stack the large balls and then began adding the finishing touches. His snowman had black coal eyes, a bright orange carrot nose, and a row of buttons for a smile. On his head rested the straw hat. Eric was pleased with his work and was glad that the sun would come out to keep the cheerful snowman warm. He could stay outdoors and play with the snowman all day.

For a variation on the activity, post the story along with a list of possible conclusions. Encourage each student to read the story, secretly select the conclusion he thinks is appropriate, and make a note of it on a piece of paper. At the end of the day, read the story aloud and poll students for their answer choices. Reveal the correct ending. Use the poll results to determine what percentage of your students are mastering the concept.

Character And Plot Development

Although many children have a favorite storybook character, they often have a hard time developing a character when writing a story of their own. Likewise, creating a plot for a work of fiction can also seem overwhelming to young writers. The following activities will help students identify the traits of interesting characters and plots they read about while promoting the transfer of this knowledge into their written work.

Quite A Character!

Before students begin to develop characters for their writing, it may be beneficial for them to examine some popular storybook friends. Have your students discuss the traits of well-known characters such as Curious George and his friend, The Man In The Yellow Hat. What are some words to describe George? Students may respond that he gets into trouble, he doesn't think before he acts, and of course he's very curious. All these qualities have made George a predictable but well-loved character. His friend has different qualities—he's dependable, he expects George to mind him, he's always there to help George deal with a problem, but most of all he loves the little monkey. These two characters have distinct qualities that help the reader to understand and appreciate the story even more.

Use the following list of fictional characters to help your students recognize different character traits. Then have them complete the follow-up activity below for practice in creating a fictional character for their own writing.

Create A Character

After your students have become familiar with character traits, let them try their hands at creating a character or two for a writing assignment. Begin by having each student decide on the character's name(s) and physical characteristics. Use copies of the reproducible on page 88 to help the children make outlines detailing their characters. If desired, have each student make several different outlines to keep on file for story-writing activities. Your classroom will be filled with a whole cast of characters!

Lyle the crocodile	Frog and Toad
Arthur the anteater	Amelia Bedelia
Clifford® the dog	Pinocchio
Berenstain Bears	the big, bad wolf
Cat In The Hat	Miss Nelson
Cinderella	Madeline
Red Riding Hood	Peter Pan
Boy who cried wolf	Mrs. Frizzle

Character And Plot Development

Character Comparisons

No two characters can be exactly alike, but some share a few common qualities! Have your students explore the similarities and differences between two characters with the help of a Venn diagram. This activity can be done as a whole group using a Venn diagram drawn on the chalkboard, as an individual activity using a Venn diagram drawn on paper, or as a partner activity using overlapping Hula-Hoops® on the floor or table. Determine which two characters to use; then label the outer side of each circle with a different character's name. Label the intersecting part of the diagram with the word "both." Have students think of words or phrases about the characters and record (or label) their responses in the corresponding areas of the diagram. Who knows? Maybe Little Red Riding Hood had more in common with the wolf than one might think!

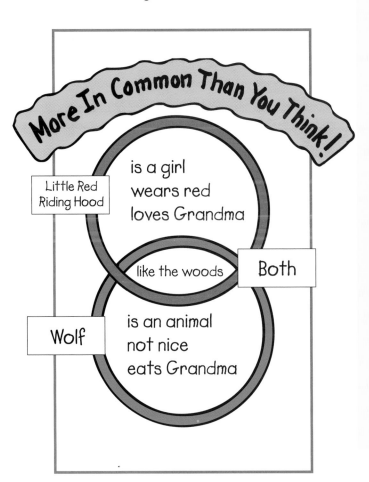

The Plot Thickens

Help your students recognize and develop plot details with the simple plot outline on page 89. It can be used to map out a story or as a tool for prewriting. When students see that there is a logical progression to a story's plot, it will help their comprehension ability as well as improve their story-writing skills.

To use the diagram, model the procedure with a story the students are familiar with, such as "The Three Little Pigs." Complete the outline to show the following ideas:

The characters are the three pigs. The problem is that they are going out into the world. It is a problem because they will each need to build a home.

The first event's problem happens when a little pig builds a house of straw and a wolf blows down the house. The problem is solved when the little pig runs to his brother's house of sticks.

The second problem happens when the wolf blows away the stick house. The problem is solved as the pigs run to the third brother's brick house.

The third problem is the wolf coming down the brick chimney. The problem is solved when the pigs work together to put an end to the wolf.

The conclusion tells us that the main problem is solved when the pigs learn that hard work is what makes for success.

The outline can also be used as a prewriting plan. Distribute an outline to each student and have him pencil in plot ideas for his story. With a plan in hand, writing should be an easier process.

Create A Character

Use this form to help you create a character
   to use in story writing.
After completing this page, draw a picture
   of your character in the picture frame.
Then keep the page on file to use in other stories.

Character's name:_____

age:_____   boy? or girl?_____

Is this character a person or an animal? _____

Things to know about this character:

he/she likes _____

he/she does not like _____

he/she lives in _____

he/she has a habit of _____

he/she likes to say _____

he/she always wants to _____

other information: _____

_____

_____

Name _____

The Plot Thickens

Use this page to outline the plot of a story you have read. Or use it to develop a story you are going to write.

Title Of Story: _____

Introduction:

? **Who** is the main character(s)? _____
_____

? **What** problem is presented? _____
_____

? **Why** is it a problem? _____
_____

1 **Event One:**
problem _____
solution _____

2 **Event Two:**
problem _____
solution _____

3 **Event Three:**
problem _____
solution _____

Conclusion:
The main problem was solved when _____
_____
_____ .

Reading And Writing Journals

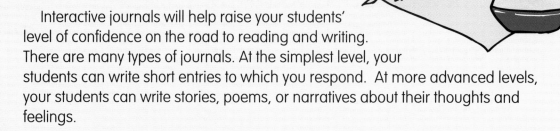

Interactive journals will help raise your students' level of confidence on the road to reading and writing. There are many types of journals. At the simplest level, your students can write short entries to which you respond. At more advanced levels, your students can write stories, poems, or narratives about their thoughts and feelings.

A journal provides a good outlet for a student to use to reflect on the events of the day, to show his reactions to a prompt, or to record his experiences with literature. Make the most out of journal time by guiding your students to write for a variety of reasons. It may be helpful to have each student divide his journal into different sections to differentiate between the types of entries he will make. Remember that each entry need not be corrected; this may lower a student's confidence level and his entries might become shorter and more labored.

One of the most common types of journal writing is the "experience entry". This is where the student keeps an account of the everyday things that happen to him. Sometimes students want to write about an exciting event that has happened at school or at home. Other times a student has something on his mind and he wants to "tell" it to his journal as a means of working through it. This section of the journal should be one that the student can write in at all times.

Some students love to write short stories and can't wait for the next writing assignment. Designate a special section in each journal for impromptu tales or story ideas for future assignments. Students may even want to keep a "work in progress" that can result in a chapter story. Reinforce to your students that they need not wait for you to make a writing assignment if they feel like writing!

Something exciting happened to me today. When I ...

Reading And Writing Journals

Getting More From Journals

Would you like to get more mileage from journal writing? Use the following activities to encourage your students to write in their journals enthusiastically and often.

Friend To Friend

Entice your students to use their journals frequently by engaging them in a pen-pal project. At the beginning of each grading period, have students draw names for classmates to correspond with. Designate a special journal section or have students use a separate notebook specifically for pen-pal correspondence. Encourage the pen pals to write to each other at least twice a week. It may help students fulfill their writing obligation if you provide a specific time for students to write to their pen pals and a later time to exchange journals. To keep the interest going, direct students to end each entry with a question for their pen pals to answer. Students will soon look forward to trading entries with their special writing partners.

Dear Pen Pal,
I ate two desserts at lunch today! Pudding is my favorite treat. What did you like best?

Learning Log

How many times have you heard a parent ask her child what he learned in school that day only to hear the reply, "I don't remember," or worse yet, "Nothing!" A quick remedy to this daily forgetfulness is having each student make a journal entry in a learning log. The learning log should be a designated part of the journal used to record skills, concepts, and information the student learned or practiced during the day. Plan for students to write in their logs as a final activity for the day. When they are greeted by their parents in the afternoon, they will have the day's events fresh in their minds and can relate information rather than shrugs.

$$\begin{array}{r} 14 \\ + 14 \\ \hline 28 \end{array}$$

noun = person, place, thing

Reading And Writing Journals

Journal Jokes

Promote an interest in journal sharing by having your students include jokes and riddles in their writing. Gather a collection of joke and riddle books for students to browse through. Ask each student to choose an amusing selection or two to copy into her journal. Set aside a special time for students to share with the class something that tickled their funny bones. Amidst all the chuckles and knee-slapping, your students will have practiced writing, reading, and speaking skills!

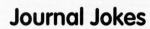

Reading Response Journals

This special entry can be used as an alternative to the traditional book report. As you finish a read-aloud story or class-assigned book, culminate the selection with small-group discussions and individual journal entries. As the class begins a new literature selection, post a list of questions that will apply to the story. Leave the list in view for students to refer to for the duration of the book. When the class has finished reading the selection, provide time for students to silently reflect on the questions. Then place students into small groups to discuss the questions aloud. Complete the activity by having each student return to his desk and write about each question in his literature-response journal. If time allows, have student volunteers share passages from their journals with their classmates. The following questions can be used with any story:

1. Did you enjoy this story? Tell why or why not.

2. What are some of the feelings you experienced during the story?

3. What part of the story did you enjoy the most?

4. Which character did you like the best? Tell why.

5. To whom would you recommend this book?

Reading And Writing Journals

Journals At Home

Often students will be absent for a few days at a stretch due to illness or family-related reasons. If you know about the situation in advance or you are able to send papers home, include the student's journal as a means of staying in touch. Write a brief note to the student asking that she write at least a few lines every day about what is happening at home, how she is feeling, or what she misses about her classmates. This will help students still feel connected to school and also keep them writing while they are away!

Point-Of-View Paragraphs

Help students understand point of view by having them get into character to write a paragraph or two. Ask each student to pretend that he is a character from a book he has read or a famous person he has learned about. Have the student write a paragraph about an assigned topic from the character's perspective. Remind the student to consider the character's background knowledge, the time period he is from, and other relevant information. If time allows, place students in small groups to share their entries and compare the different views.

Current Events

Keep your students aware of newsworthy topics by having a special journal section especially for current events. Encourage your students to scan the newspaper or listen to the news for stories that are making headlines. If national news is a little intimidating for your youngsters, have them write about local or schoolwide happenings. Since this is a fact-based entry, your students will experience a change from the fictional story writing or personal narratives. You may be surprised at how much your class knows about events in the news!

A Place For Poetry

A journal can be the perfect place for budding poets. Encourage each student to experiment with verse and different poetic forms, such as cinquains, limericks, couplets, haiku, and shape poems. If students are reluctant to read their creations to the class, encourage them to let you have a peek. Or assign each child a personal poetry pal to share her work with. Remember that a journal can be a very personal thing, and poetry can be the most personal entry of all!

The Role Of The Parents

An important part of any reading program is getting parents involved. It is often necessary to emphasize to parents that reading is not an isolated school skill; it should be practiced at home and it should be an enjoyable experience. Use the following activities to let parents know that reading is a top priority. Your partnership with them will help produce a classroom full of eager readers.

I Read, You Read

Most parents will agree on the importance of reading to young children, whether in the form of a bedtime story or a library book that they have chosen together. Let your parents know that even though their children are reading for themselves, it is still beneficial for adults to continue to read to youngsters. As children become independent readers, they still need to hear literature read aloud to help improve their listening skills and vocabulary. And as most parents will tell you, a special closeness occurs when a book is shared.

Let your parents know that you will provide a recommended reading list or perhaps loan a few of your books for the purpose of parent-child reading time. Grade-level books can provide a chance for the parent to read a few pages and then for the child to read part of the selection. More challenging books can be a pure listening experience for the child and will be just as beneficial to the reading process. Whatever families select as literature, emphasize that they should read, read, read!

Reading All Around

Parents may not realize it, but there is plenty of reading material all around. Encourage parents to take advantage of cereal-box print by asking, "What does it say about the enclosed prize?" or inquiring, "How many calories are in a serving?" There is print in supermarkets, on billboards, and in restaurants. Remind parents that a mini reading session can take place just about anywhere!

Parent Newsletter

Keeping parents informed of reading instruction in the classroom can help you bridge the home-school connection. A monthly classroom newsletter can provide parents with tips and skills to reinforce reading at home. Use the reproducible newsletter on page 96 to let parents know what specific skills, letter sounds, or vocabulary you will be reinforcing. You may wish to include a list of children's books that will enhance your studies at school.

The newsletter is a great place to include reading materials for parents and children to share. Feature a few stories or poems written by students that will make good family reading.

Your newsletter can also introduce reading activities for families to complete together. Suggest some of the following projects that will reinforce reading skills in a fun-filled way.

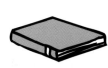

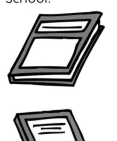

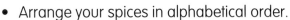
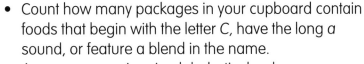

- Count how many packages in your cupboard contain foods that begin with the letter C, have the long *a* sound, or feature a blend in the name.
- Arrange your spices in alphabetical order.
- Write a note to your child telling him about your day. Ask him to write you a note in response.
- Find the describing words featured on your shampoo, conditioner, or toothpaste.
- Find a comic in the funny pages that makes you both laugh.
- Check the newspaper for the forecast.
- Read a recipe together and try it out later in the week.
- Take turns reading street signs or billboards as you drive.
- Read the nutrition labels together before you buy snacks. Find a healthful choice.
- Read the television listings together instead of changing channels to see what's on.

Reading In The News

Teacher: _____ Date: _____

Tips And Skills

Activities And Projects

Spotlight On...

Stories To Read Together